Fly High
Pupil's Book
1
T0386084

Danae Kozanoglou

Contents

Hello!

Hello. I'm Cabu.
What's your name?

In the jungle

1 **Listen and point. Then say.** 

lion

elephant

parrot

boy

girl

2 **Look and listen.** 

3 **Listen again and say.** 

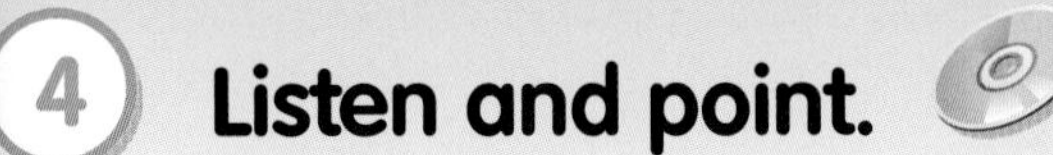

4 Listen and point.

1

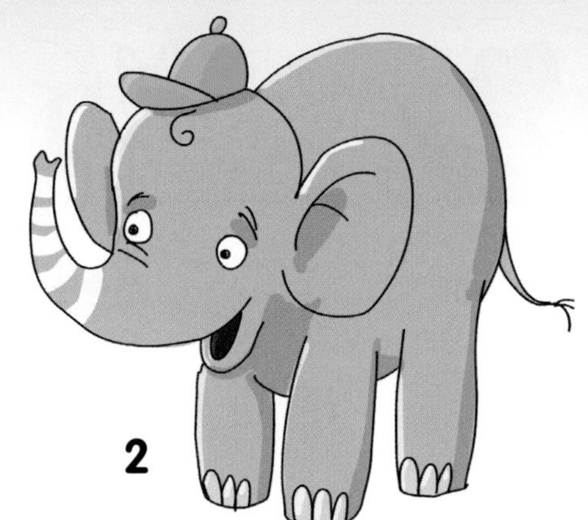

2

3

5 Listen and say. 

Hello. I'm Cabu.
I'm a lion. What's
your name?

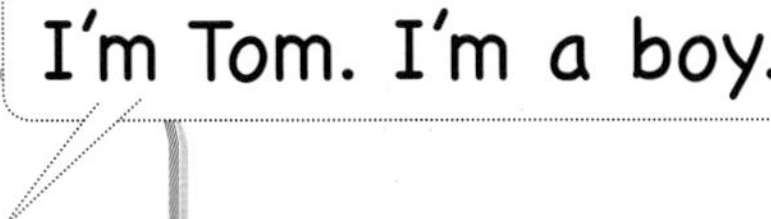
I'm Tom. I'm a boy.

6 Draw and say.

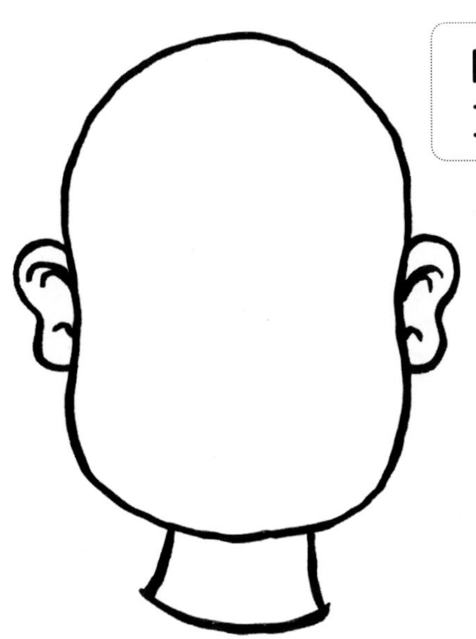

Hello. I'm ...
I'm a ...

7 Listen and point. Then say. 

banana

flower

bee

hippo

8 Look and listen.

1

2

3

9 Listen again and say. 

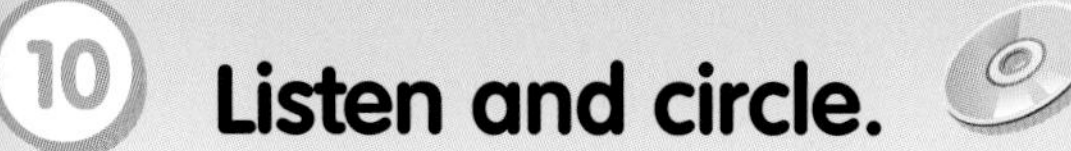

10 Listen and circle.

1

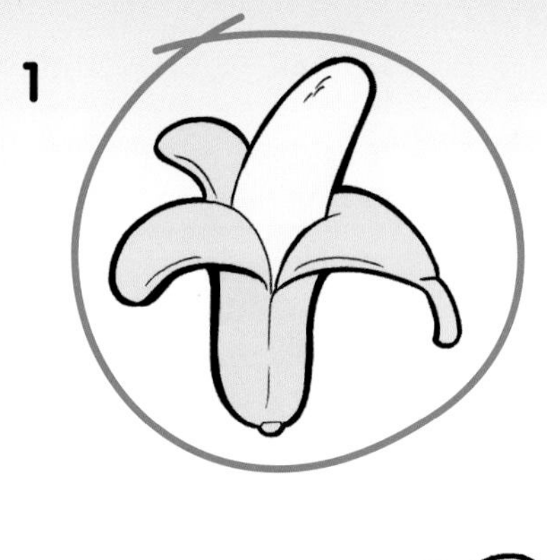

2

3

4

5

6

11 Listen and point. Then sing.

Look, an elephant and a bee.

2 Colours (1)

1 Listen and point. Then say.

yellow blue red green

2 Look and listen.

3 Listen again and say.

4 Listen and colour.

1

2

3

4

5 Point and say.

It's yellow.

6 Play.

Look, it's red.
Look, it's blue.

7 Listen and point. Then sing.

8 Colour and say.

It's red and yellow.

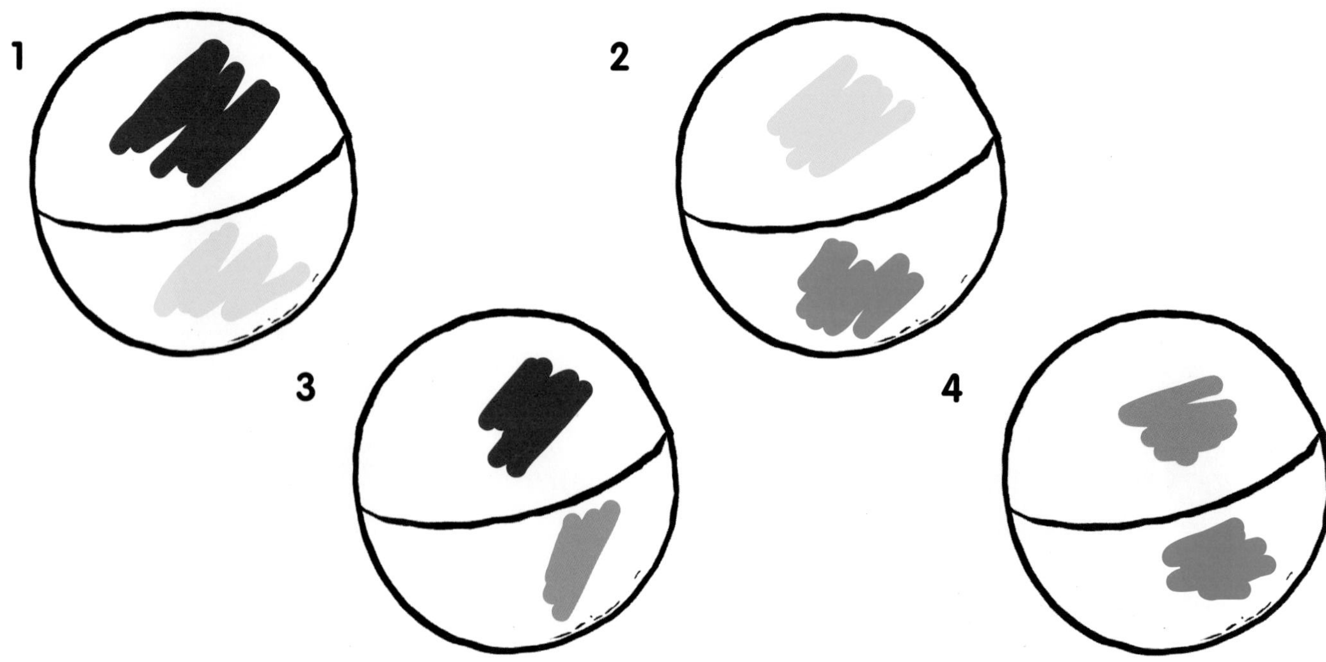
1
2
3
4

Listen and answer yes or no.

1

2

3

4
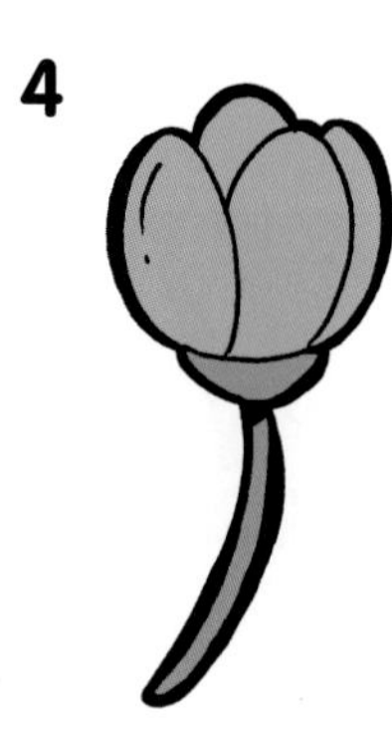

5

Play.

Is it yellow?

No.

3 Numbers 1–5

1 Listen and point. Then say.

one	two	three	four	five

2 Look and listen.

1

2

3

4

3 Listen again and say.

4 **Listen and circle.**

5 **Point and say.** 3 bees.

6 **Draw and colour. Then match.**

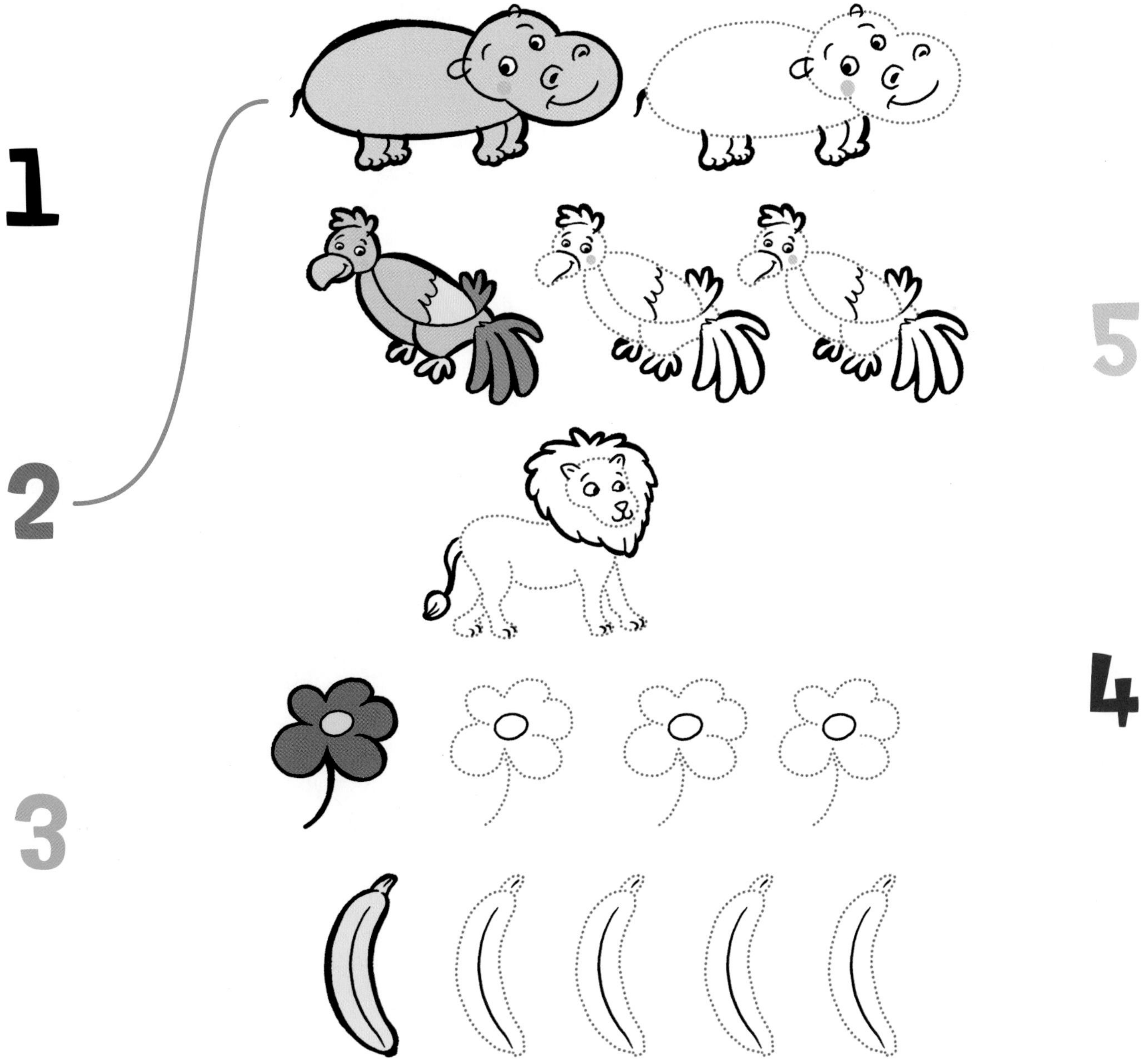

1

5

2

4

3

7 Listen and stick. Then sing. 

8 Look and count. Then match and say.

4 parrots.

1 2 3 4 5

9 Play.

1, 2 ...

4

In the classroom

1 Listen and point. Then say.

a b c

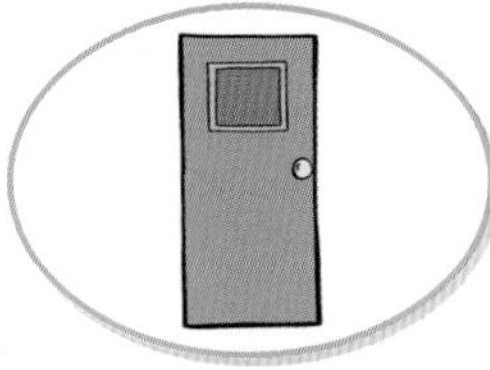

teacher desk chair book door

2 Look and listen.

1

2

3

4

3 Listen again and say.

4 Listen and circle.

1
2
3
4
5

5 Point and say.

Here's your chair.

6 Play.

Here's your desk.

7 Listen and point. Then sing.

1

2

3

8 Point and say.

Trumpet, here's your chair.

9 Find and count. Then say.

5 bananas.

10 Draw and colour. Then say.

It's a desk. It's green and yellow.

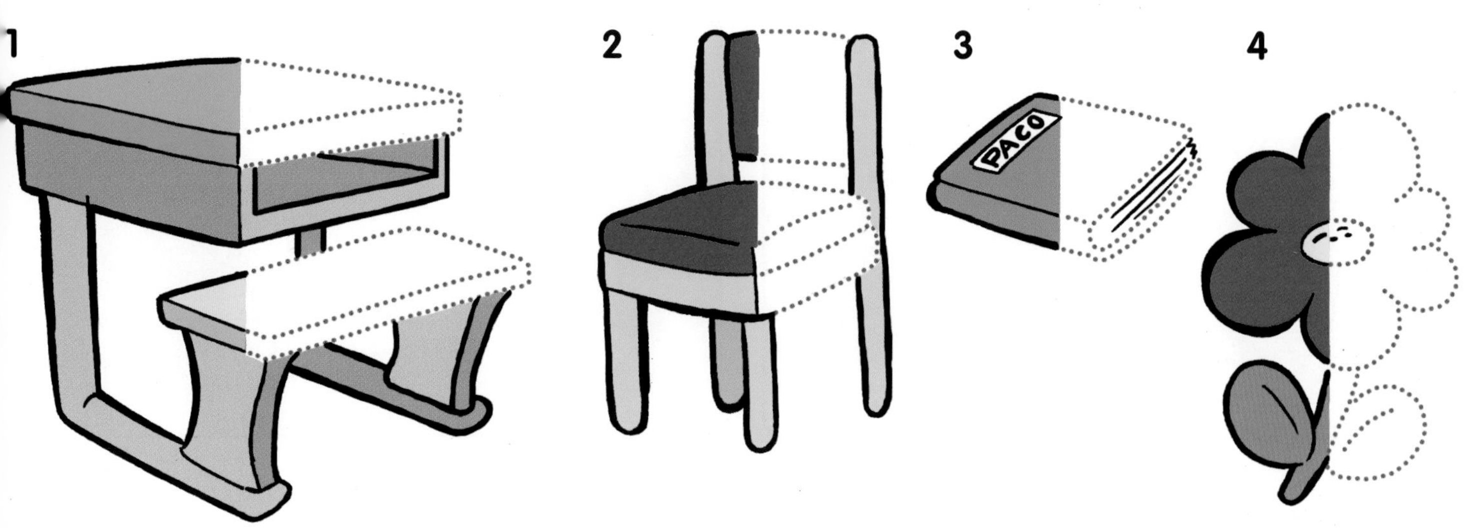
1
2
3
PACO
4

School things

1 **Listen and point. Then say.** 

bag

pencil

crayon

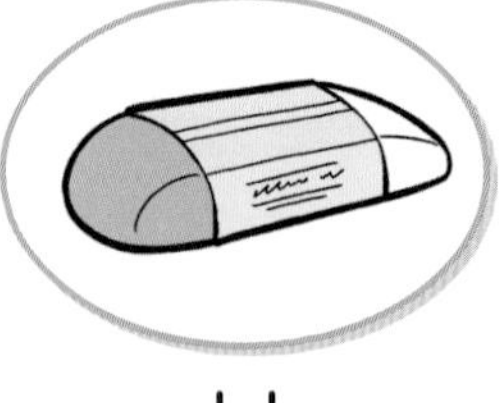
rubber

2 **Look and listen.**

3 **Listen again and say.** 

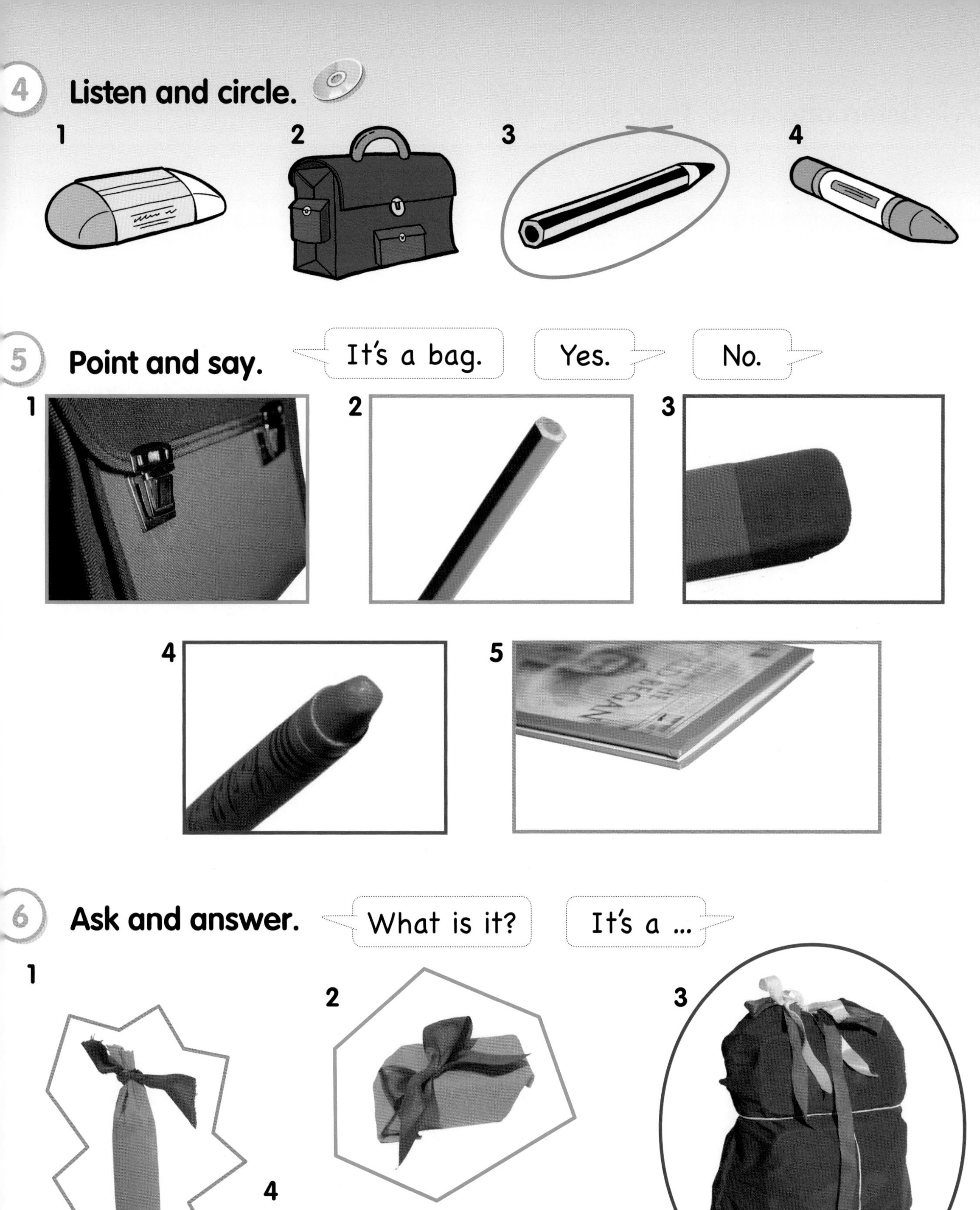

4 Listen and circle.
1
2
3
4
5 Point and say.
It's a bag.
Yes.
No.
1
2
3
4
5
6 Ask and answer.
What is it?
It's a ...
1
2
3
4

7 Listen and stick. Then sing.

8 Draw and colour. Then say.

It's a pencil. It's blue.

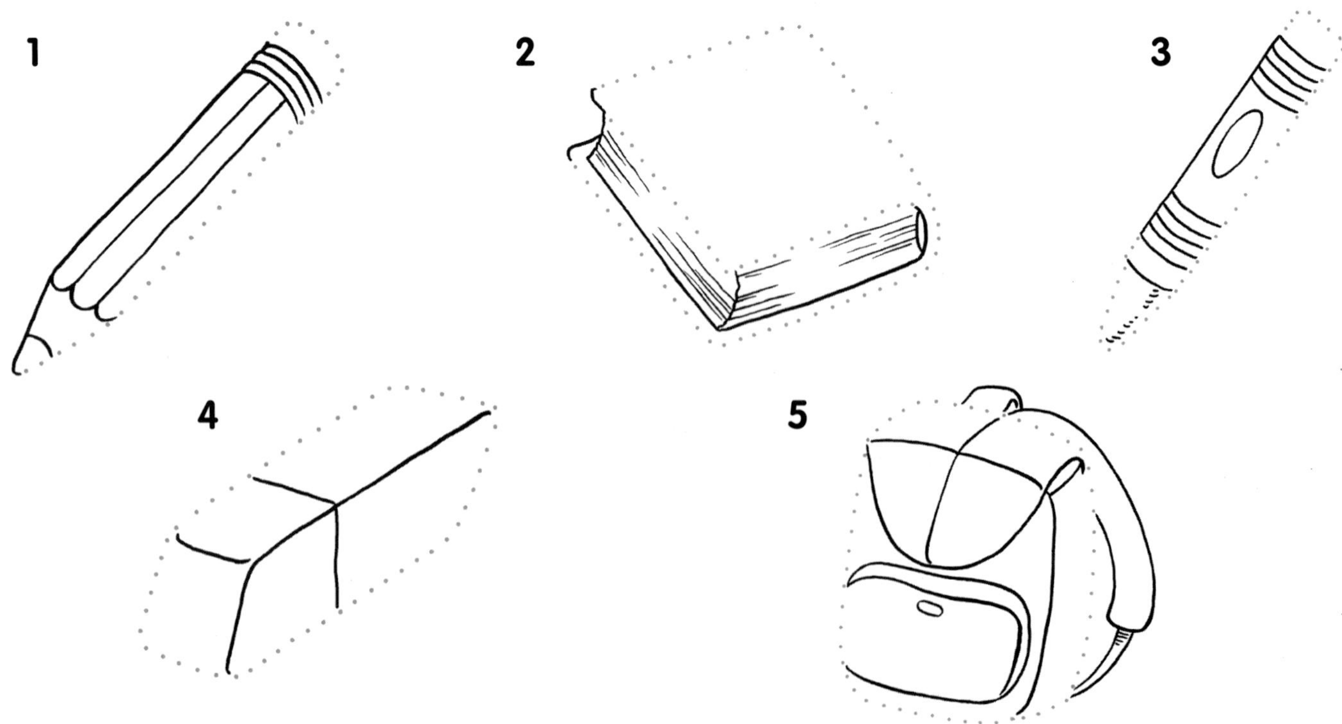
1
2
3
4
5

9 Listen and circle.

1 2 3 4 5

10 Point, ask and answer.

Is it a pencil?

Yes.

11 Play.

Is it a crayon?
No.
MYTHS AND LEGENDS
HOW THE

6

Classroom actions

1 **Listen and point. Then say.** 

sit down | stand up | clap | turn around

2 **Look and listen.**

1

2

3

4

3 **Listen again and say.** 

4 Listen and number.

a

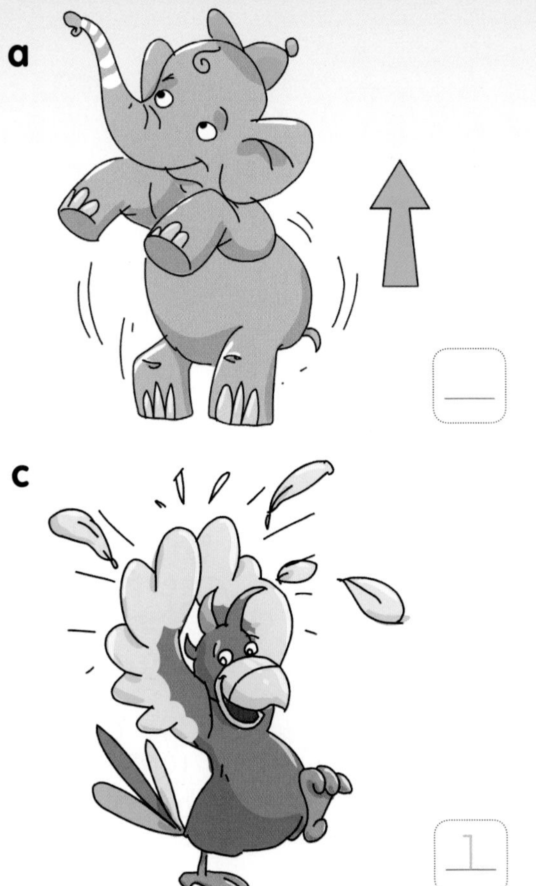

b

c

d

1

5 Point and say.

6 Play.

Stand up.

7 Listen and point. Then sing.

8 Sing and do.

9 Point and say.

Sit down.

1
2
3
4
5

10 Draw and colour. Then say.

1

2

11 Guess and say.

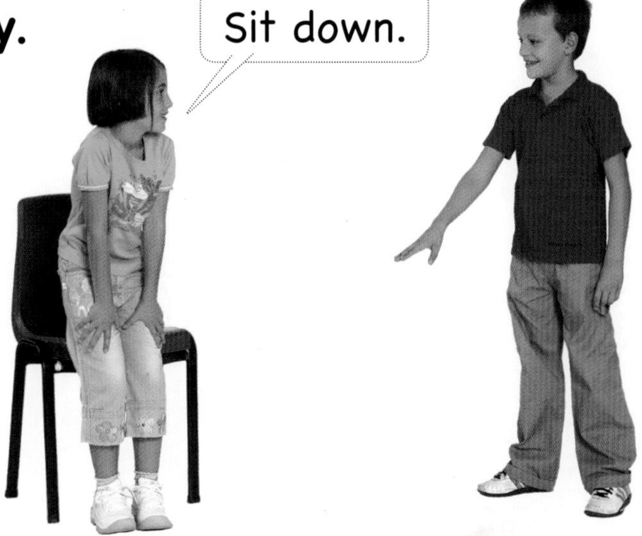
Sit down.

12 Listen and do.

JUNGLE FUN 1

1 Play.

1
2
3
4

5

My alphabet a b c

① **Listen and repeat. Then circle.**

/eɪ/ a   /biː/ b   /siː/ c

/æ/ apple   /b/ ball   /k/ car

② **Find and circle.**

/æ/	a b c a a c b c a b a c a b a
	A B A C B A C B A C A B A A C
/b/	b a c b a b b c a b c b a b c
	B C A B C B B A A B C B C A B
/k/	c a c b a c b c a b c c a b c
	C A C B C C A C B A A C B C A

3 Match and draw. Then colour.

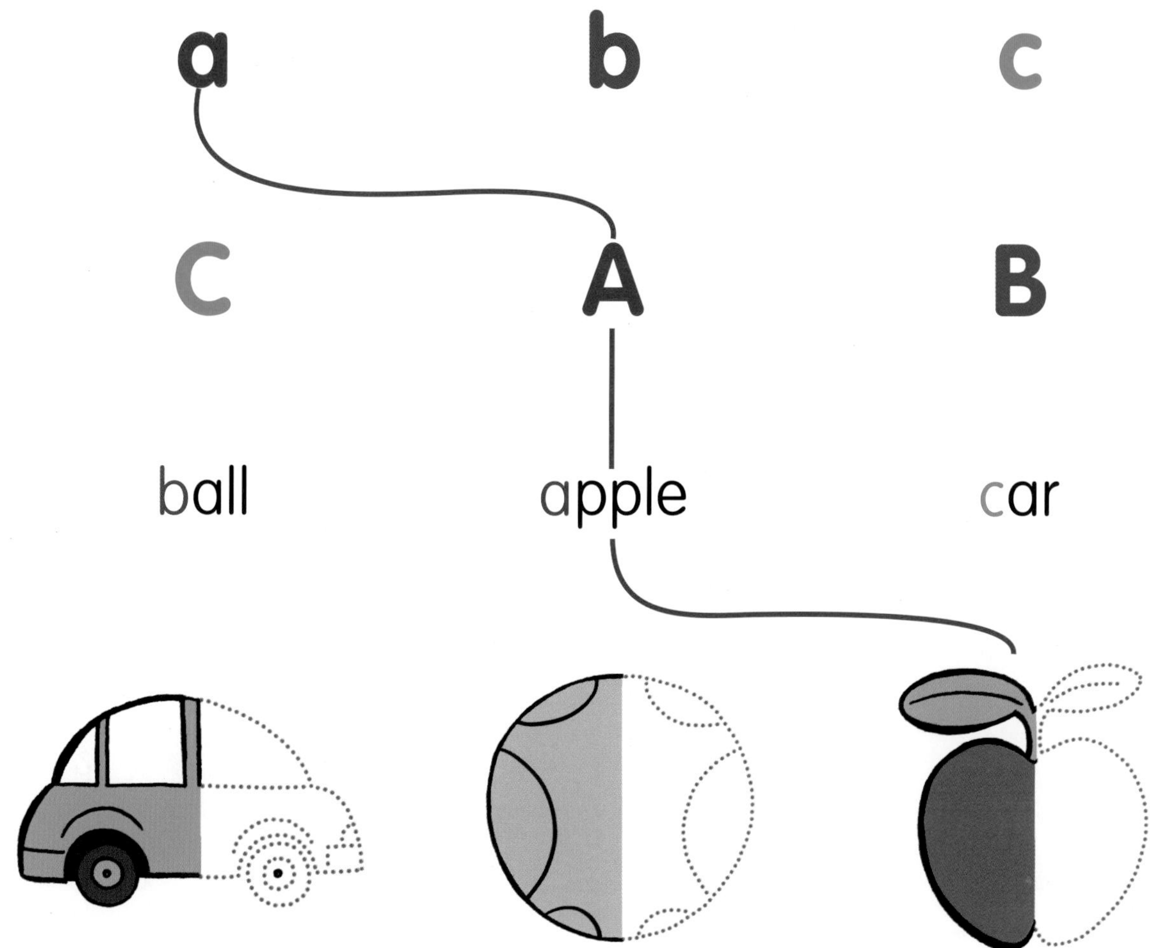

a
b
c
C
A
B
ball
apple
car

4 Look and colour.

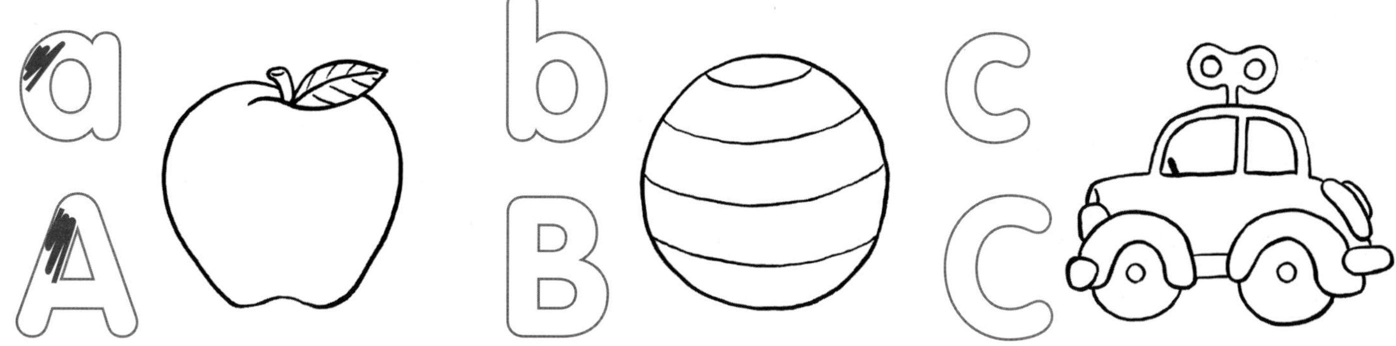

a
A
b
B
c
C

5 Chant.

A B C D E F G H I J K L M N O P Q R S T U V W X Y Z
a b c d e f g h i j k l m n o p q r s t u v w x y z

7 Family

1 Listen and point. Then say.

mum dad brother sister me

2 Look and listen.

1
Hello!

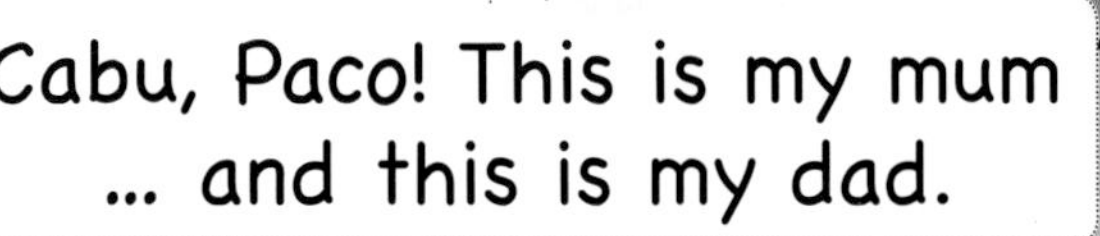
Cabu, Paco! This is my mum
... and this is my dad.

2
This is my brother, Bill.
Hello!

3
What?
Oh ... and this is my sister Elli.
Hello!

4
And this is me!

3 Listen again and say.

4 Listen and number.

1

5 Point and say.

This is my mum.

6 Draw your family and say.

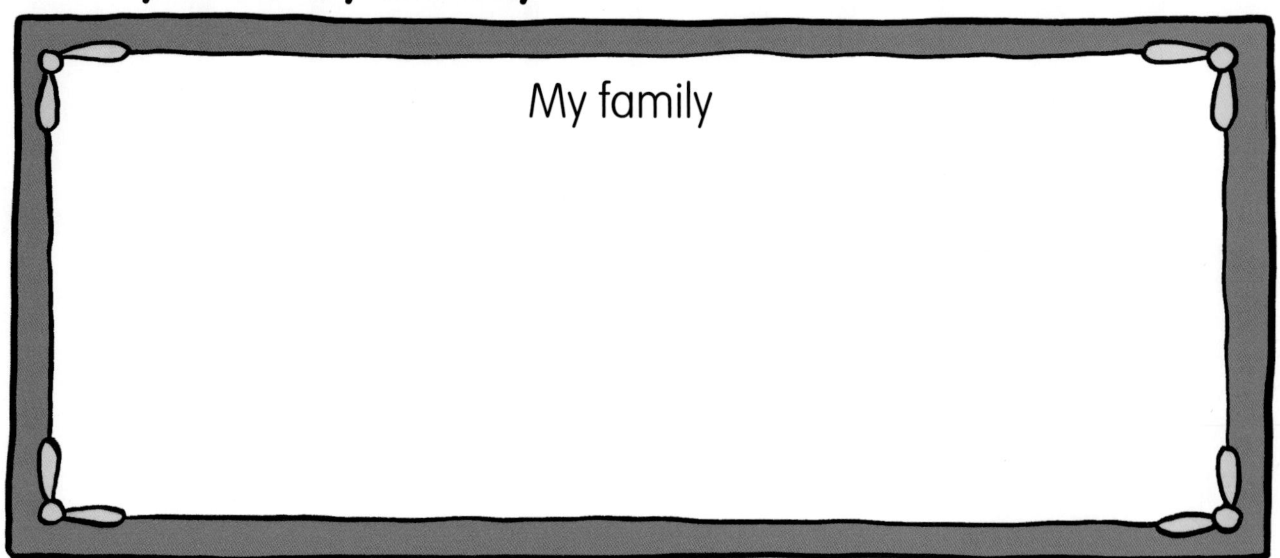
My family

7 Listen and stick. Then sing.

This is my mum.
Hello, hello.
This is my dad.
Hello, hello.

Mum and Dad,
Mum and Dad,
Mum and Dad,
Hello, hello.

This is my brother.
Hello, hello.
This is my sister.
Hello, hello.

Brother and sister
Brother and sister
Brother and sister
Hello, hello!

8 Listen and say yes or no.

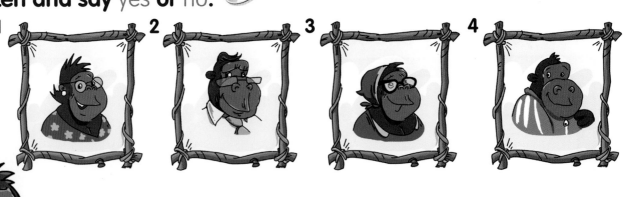

1
2
3
4

9 Find and say.

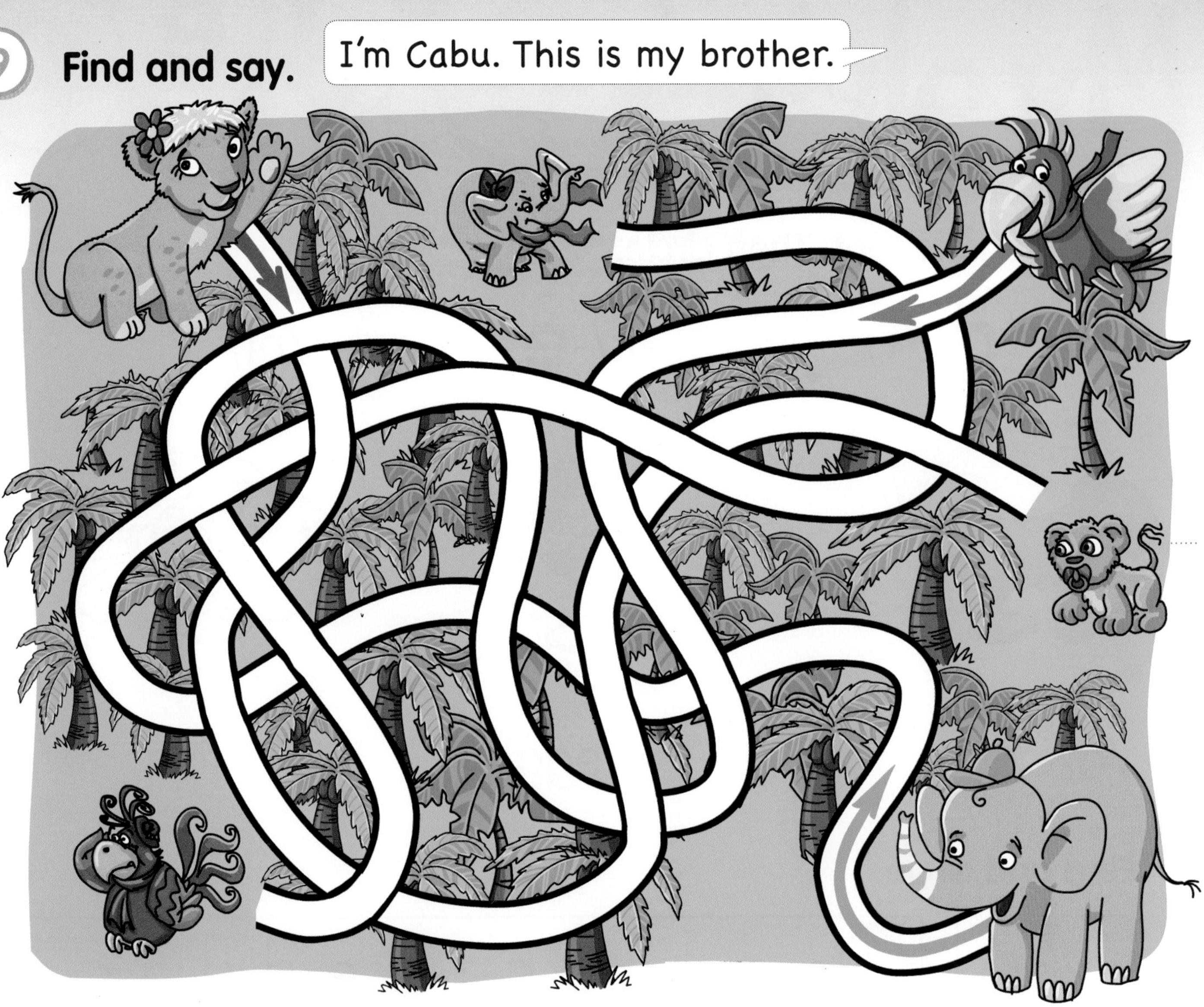

I'm Cabu. This is my brother.

10 Play.

This is my family.

My alphabet d e f

1 Listen and repeat. Then circle.

/diː/ d   /iː/ e   /ef/ f

/d/ dog   /e/ egg   /f/ fish

2 Find and circle.

/d/	d e d a f d c f d e d d a c d
	D A C D D B C D A D C B D A D
/e/	e a e b c e e d e b e f a e f
	E C A E C F E A E D C E C A E
/f/	f e d f a f f c f b c f a d f
	F A F B E F A D F A E F F C F

3 Match and draw. Then colour.

d
e
f
F
D
E

4 Match and say.

a b c d e f

5 Chant.

A B C D E F G H I J K L M N O P Q R S T U V W X Y Z
a b c d e f g h i j k l m n o p q r s t u v w x y z

8 Toys

1 Listen and point. Then say.

train

plane

bike

guitar

2 Look and listen.

1
One, two, three. Go!

2

Look! I've got a train.

3
Look! I've got a plane!

4
I've got a bike ...
and a guitar!

3 Listen again and say.

4 Listen and circle.

1

2

3

4

5 Point and say.

Look! I've got a guitar.

1

2

3

4

5

6

6 Listen and stick. Then sing. 

I've got a bike.
I've got a train.

I've got a ball
And I've got a plane.

I've got a guitar!

A yellow bike.
A red train.
A green ball.
A blue plane.
And a guitar!

 Listen and colour. 

1

2

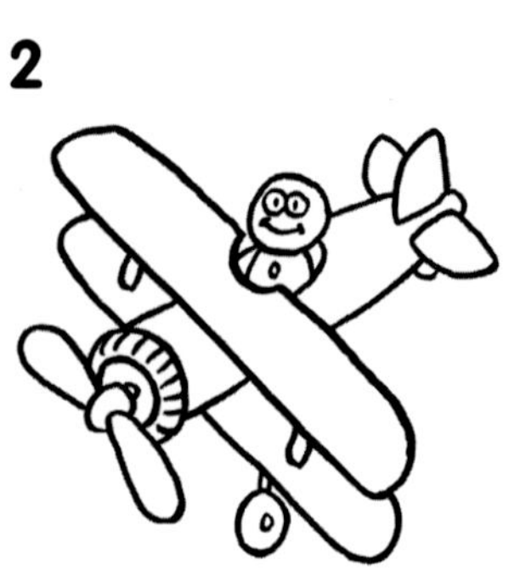

3

4

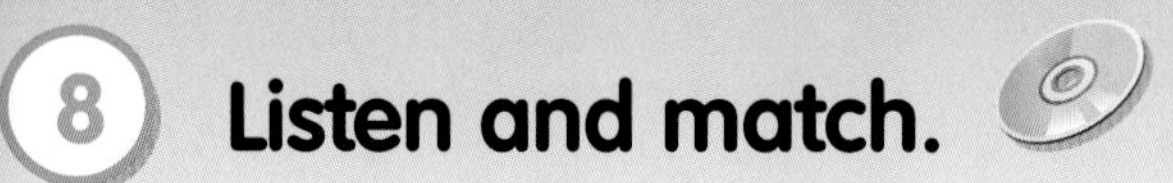

8 Listen and match.

1
2
3
4
5
a
b
c
d
e

9 Draw, colour and say.

My favourite toy is my...

My alphabet g h i

① **Listen and repeat. Then circle.**

/dʒiː/ g

/eɪtʃ/ h

/aɪ/ i

/g/ goat

/h/ horse

/ɪ/ insect

② **Find and circle.**

/g/	g d g e f g c g g b h g i c g
	G A C G D B C G H G I G G E G
/h/	h a h b c h e d f h e h g h h
	H C A D H F E H I H H E H G E
/ɪ/	i e d f i h i g f i c i a i i
	I I F B E I A D I I H G I C I

3 Match and colour.

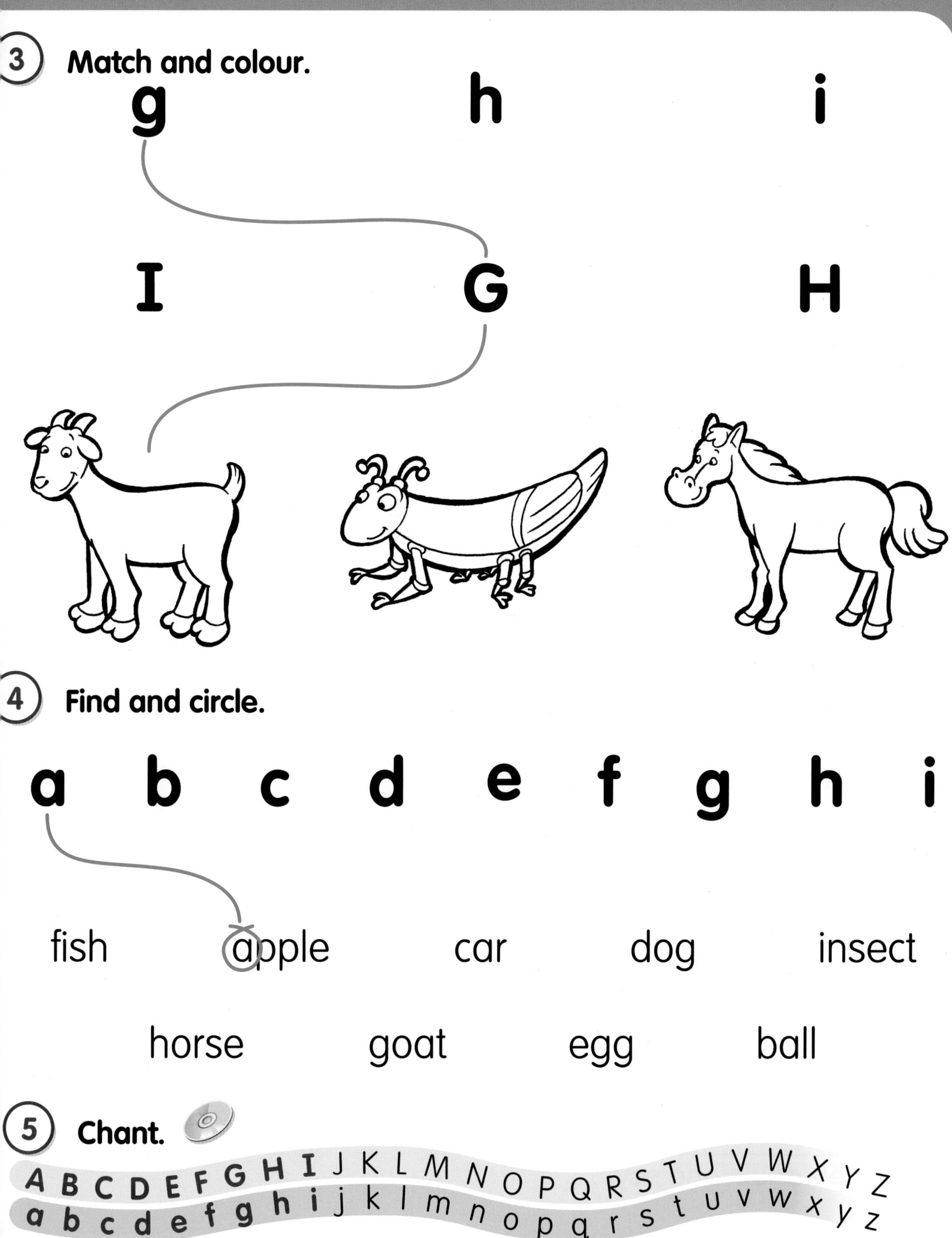

g h i
I G H

4 Find and circle.

a b c d e f g h i

fish apple car dog insect

horse goat egg ball

5 Chant.

A B C D E F G H I J K L M N O P Q R S T U V W X Y Z
a b c d e f g h i j k l m n o p q r s t u v w x y z

9 Colours (2)

1 **Listen and point. Then say.** 

pink

black

orange

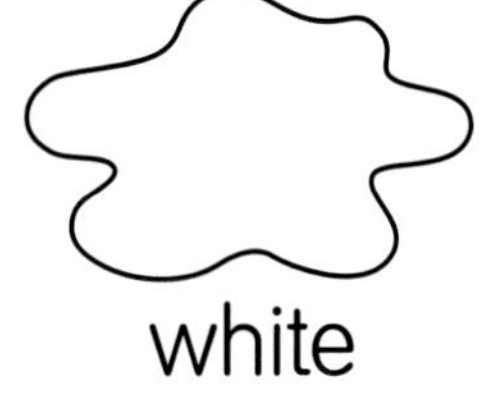
white

2 **Look and listen.**

1
Cabu! Trumpet! Look! I can see a bird! A pink bird!

2

Trumpet! Look! A black bike! I can see a black bike.

And I can see an orange bike. Look!

3
Trumpet! Look! I can see a bag. A white bag!
Yum, yum.

3 **Listen again and say.** 

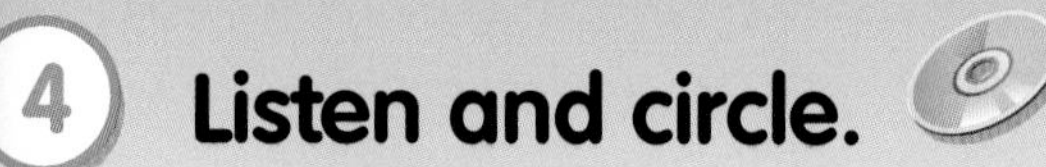

4 Listen and circle.

1 2 3 4

5 Point and say.

I can see a pink bird.

6 Colour and say.

I can see …

1

2

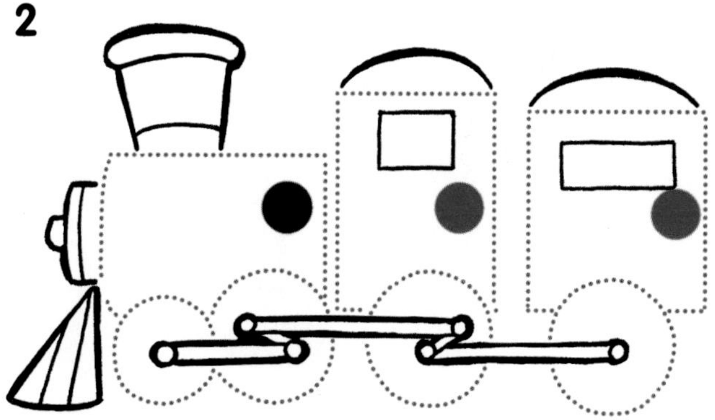

3

4

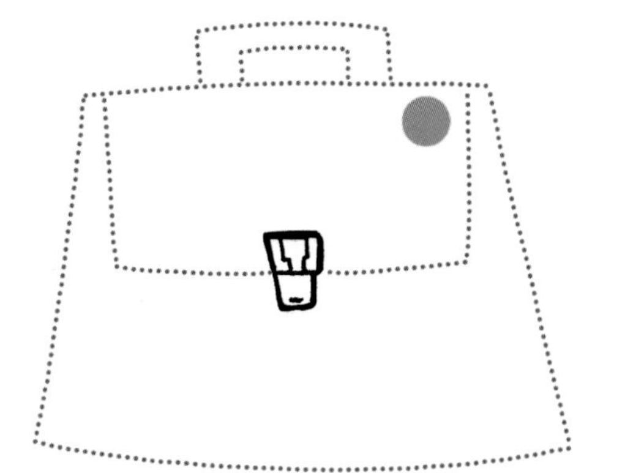

7 Listen and stick. Then sing. 

Look! I can see two bags.
A yellow bag, an orange bag.

I can see a black bird.
I can see a white bird too!

Look! I can see two balls.
A big blue ball, a small red ball.

I can see a green fish.
I can see a pink fish too!

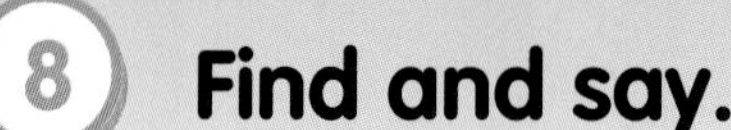

8 Find and say.

I can see …

9 Match and say.

I'm Miss Maru. My favourite colour is orange.

My alphabet j k l

1 **Listen and repeat. Then circle.**

/dʒei/ j

/keɪ/ k

/el/ l

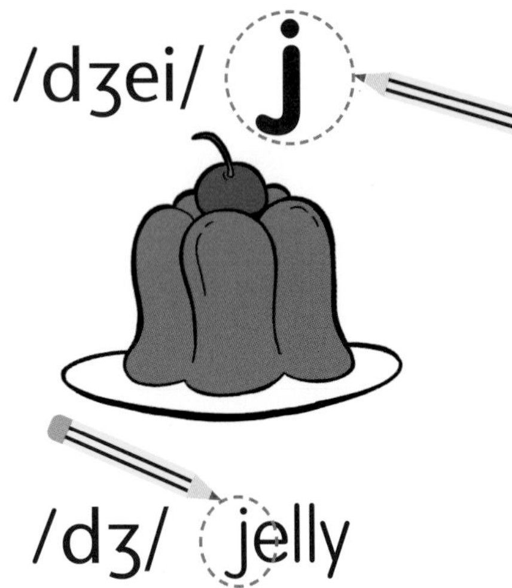

/dʒ/ jelly

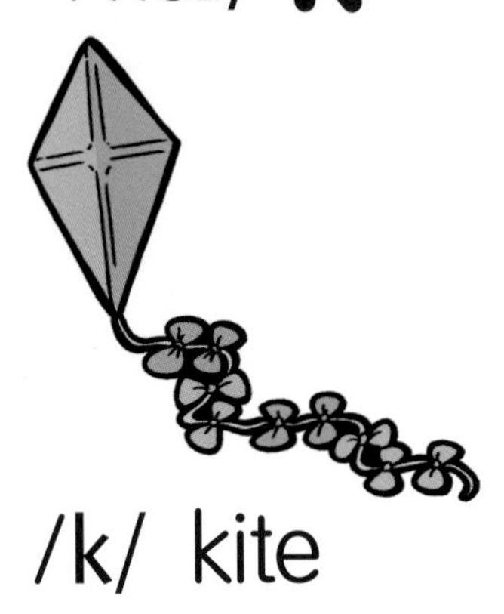

/k/ kite

/l/ lorry

2 **Find and circle.**

/dʒ/	j h g j f j c f j k j l j j d
	J H C J I B J K J J D E J F J
/k/	k h k c k i k j d k f k k f
	K C K E K F K A K J K L C K J
/l/	l e l f l k l h l b l g j d l
	L H L K E L L D F L E C L J L

3 Find and circle.

j
k
l
kite
L
j
lorry
K
l
J
k

4 Match and write. Then say.

d
a b c
d e f
g h i
j k l

5 Chant.

A B C D E F G H I J K L M N O P Q R S T U V W X Y Z

a b c d e f g h i j k l m n o p q r s t u v w x y z

10

Numbers 6–10

1 Listen and point. Then say. 

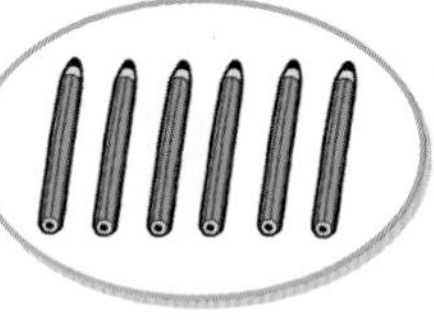
six

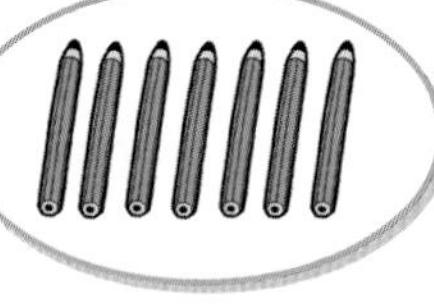
seven

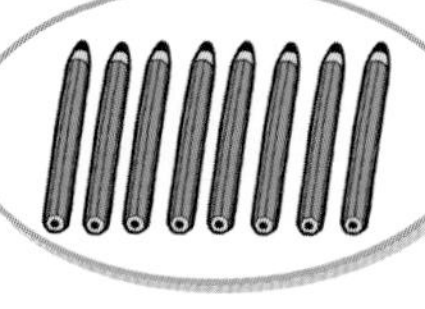
eight

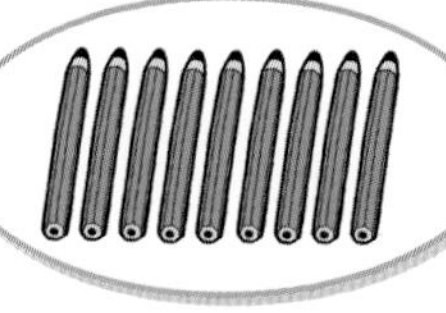
nine

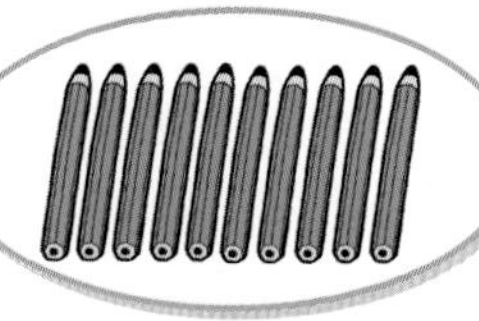
ten

2 Look and listen. 

1
Look! Six pencils. 1, 2, 3, 4, 5, 6.
6
Six.

2
Seven, eight. 1, 2, 3, 4, 5, 6, 7, 8
7
8
Yes, seven, eight.
Very good!

3
Nine.
9
Ten.
10

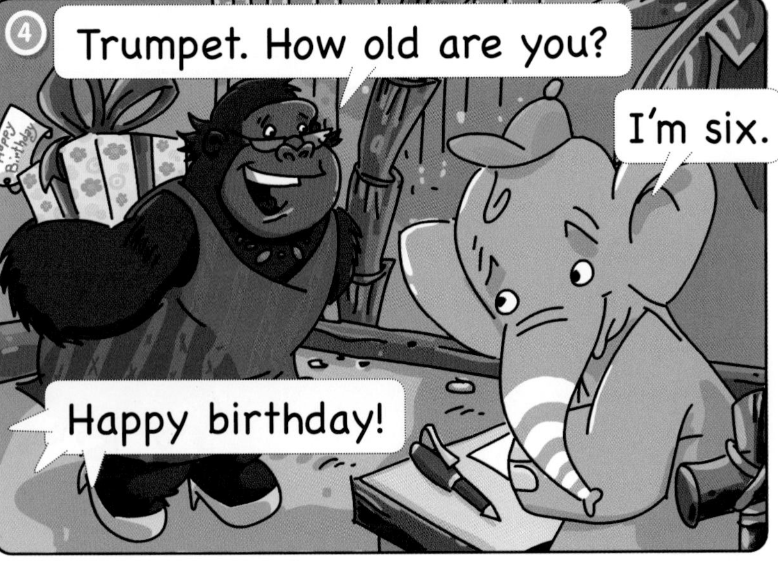
4
Trumpet. How old are you?
I'm six.
Happy birthday!

3 Listen again and say. 

4 Match and say.

Six apples.

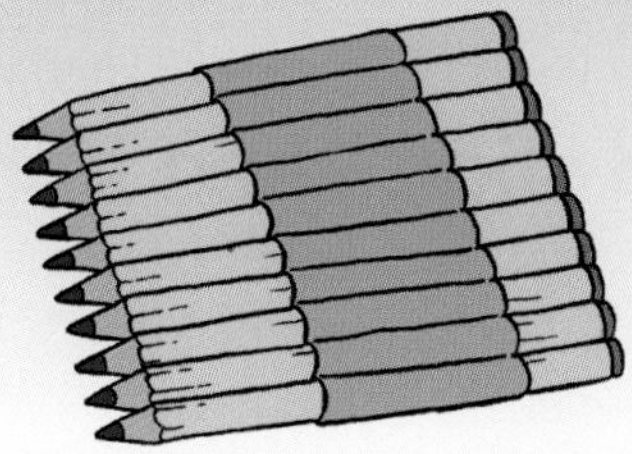

6

7

8

9

10

5 Count and write.

1
__
3
__
5
__
__
8
__
10

6 Guess and say.

Four.

No.

Five.

Yes.

7 Listen and stick. Then sing. 

Look, look!
Ten red apples.
Ten green apples.
Crunch! Crunch!

Look, look!
Nine red apples.
Nine green apples.
Crunch! Crunch!

Look, look!
Eight red apples.
Eight green apples.
Crunch! Crunch!

Look, look!
Seven red apples.
Seven green apples.
Crunch! Crunch!

Look, look!
Six red apples.
Six green apples.
On the apple tree!

8 **Find and count. Then say.**

Look! Two fish.

9 **Write and draw. Then colour.**

How old are you?

HAPPY BIRTHDAY

10 **Say.**

How old are you?

I'm six.

Happy Birthday!

Thank you.

My alphabet m n o

1 **Listen and repeat. Then circle.**

/em/ **m**

/en/ **n**

/əʊ/ **o**

/m/ monkey

/n/ nurse

/ɒ/ orange

2 **Find and circle.**

/m/	m k j m a n m c m g m m i m o
	M A C D M B C M A M C M M A M
/n/	n a n e m c n n o n n j m h n
	N C A N N F E A N D C N N A N
/ɒ/	o e a o o c g o f o c o a o n
	O A O B E O A D O A E O O C O

3 Match and say.

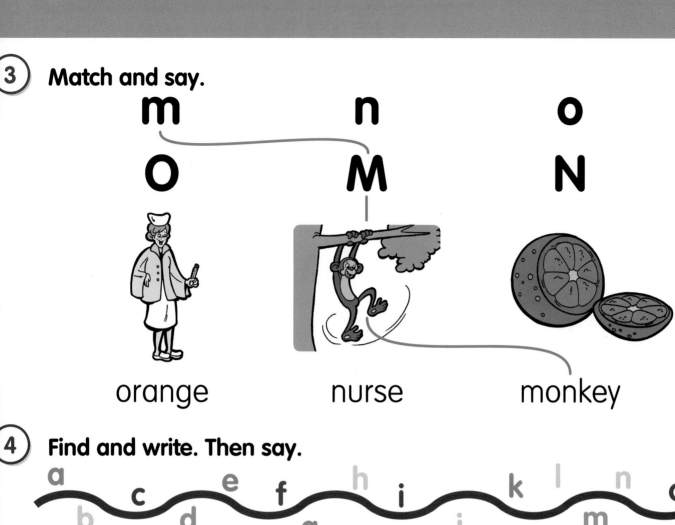

m n o

O M N

orange nurse monkey

4 Find and write. Then say.

a b c d e f g h i j k l m n o

a
d
g
j
m

5 Chant.

A B C D E F G H I J K L M N O P Q R S T U V W X Y Z

a b c d e f g h i j k l m n o p q r s t u v w x y z

JUNGLE FUN 2

1. **Look at the walls. Count and say.**

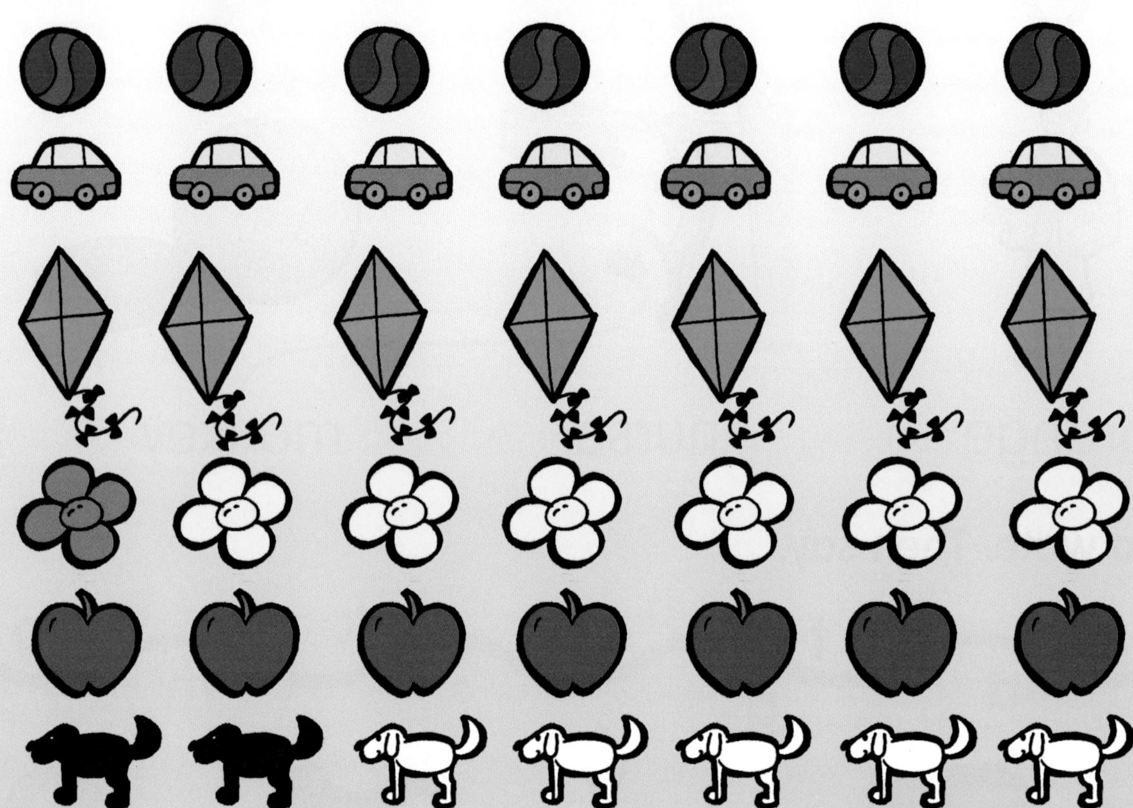

2 **Draw your family and say.**

3 **Draw your toys and say.**

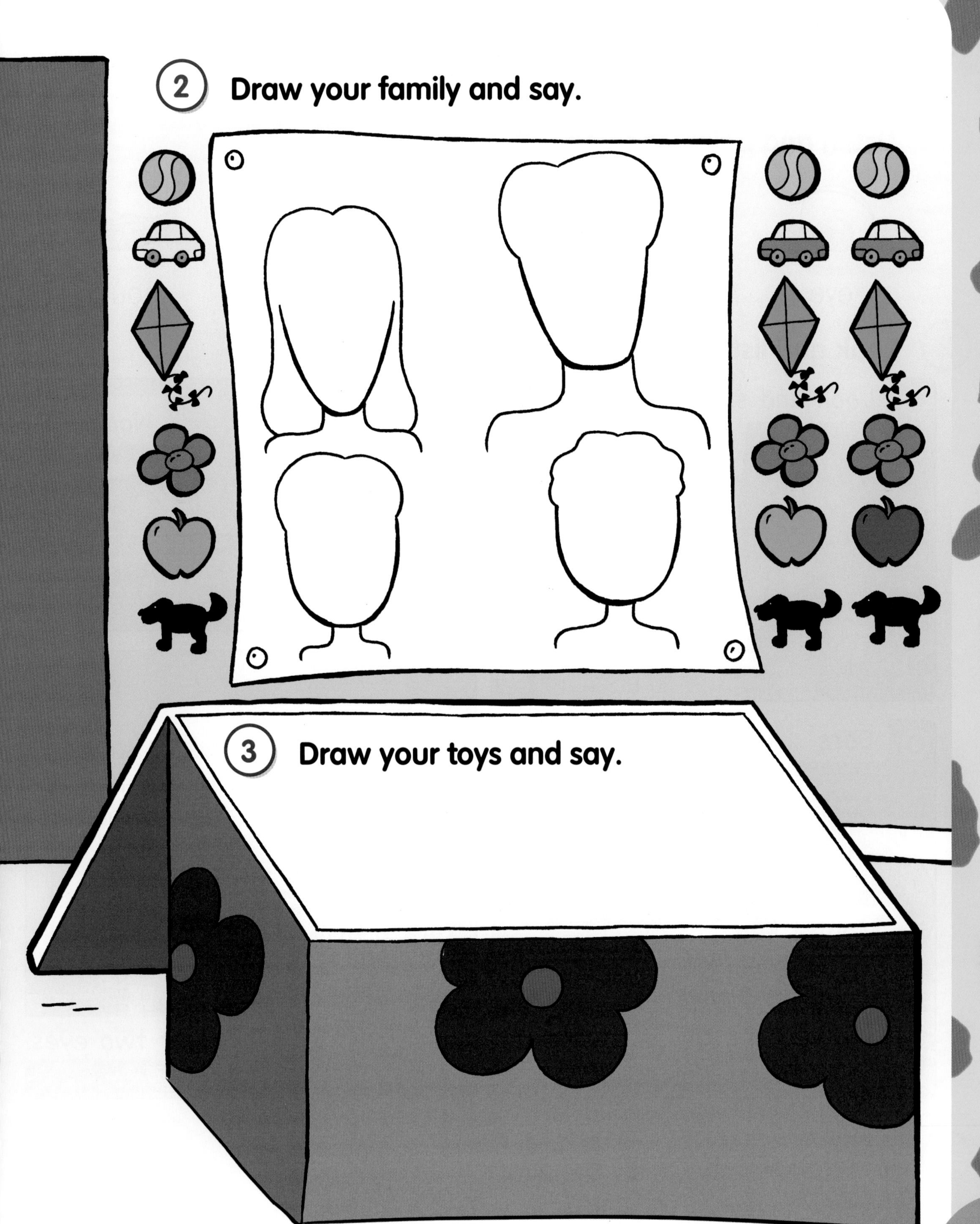

11 Face

1 Listen and point. Then say.

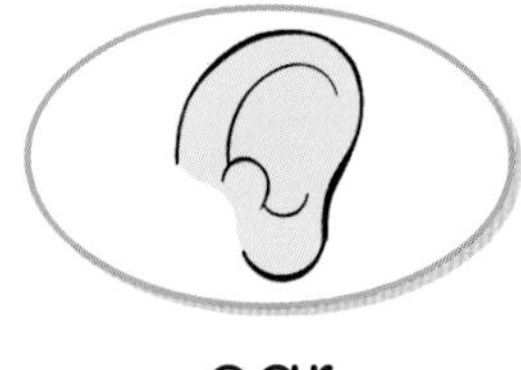

eye nose ear mouth

2 Look and listen.

1
Look and say. Eyes!
Eyes.

2
Nose!
Nose.

3
Ears ... and mouth!
Mouth!
Ears.

4
Oh! I've got a nose.
I've got two ears and a mouth.
I've got two eyes.

3 Listen again and say.

4 Listen and number.

a
b
c
d
1

5 Point and say.

've got two ears.

6 Play.

Trumpet says touch your nose.

7 Listen and match. Then sing.

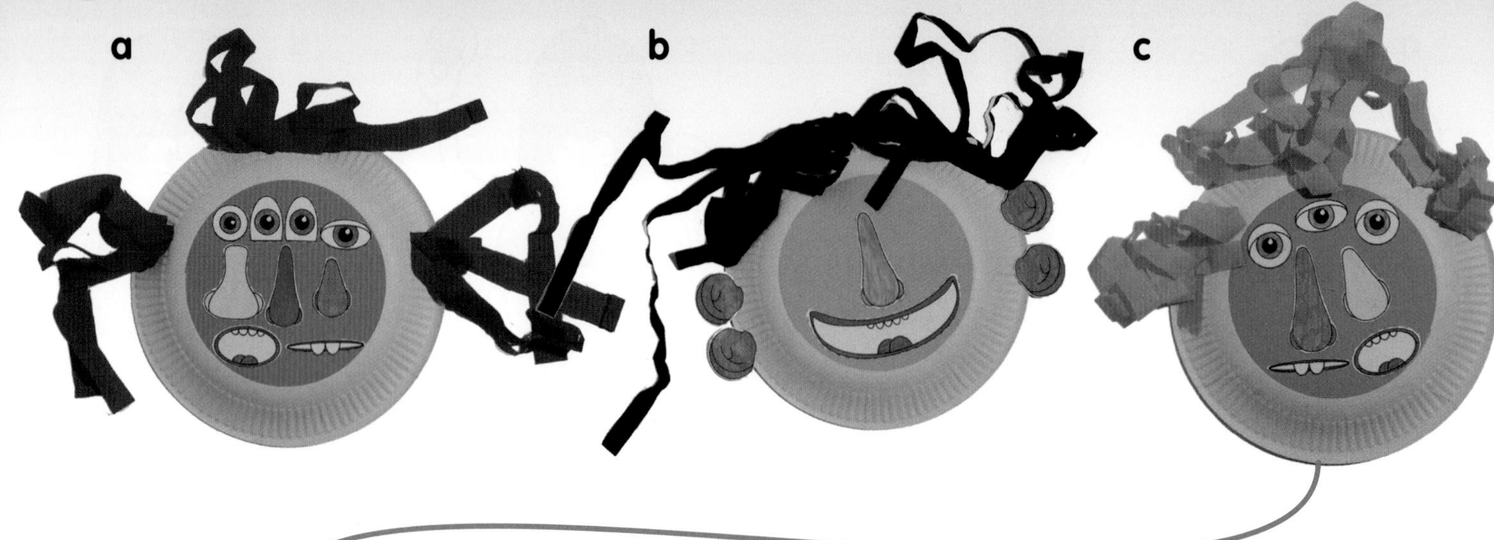
a
b
c

1 Look! Look!
I've got three eyes
And two noses
And two mouths.

2 Look! Look!
I've got four eyes
And three noses
And two mouths.

3 Look! Look!
I've got four ears
And one nose
And one mouth.

8 Draw and colour. Then say.

9 Look and say.

I can see an eye.

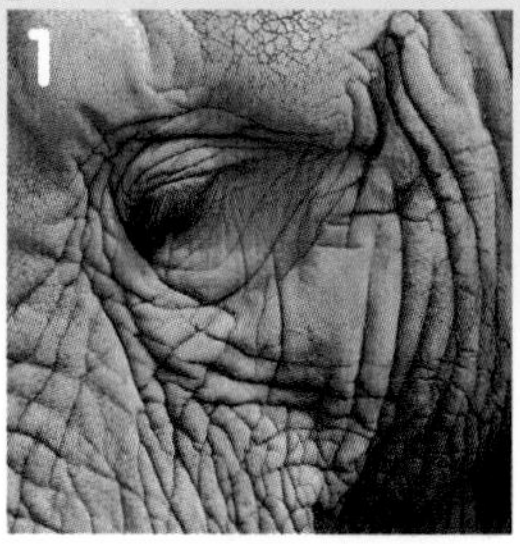

2

3

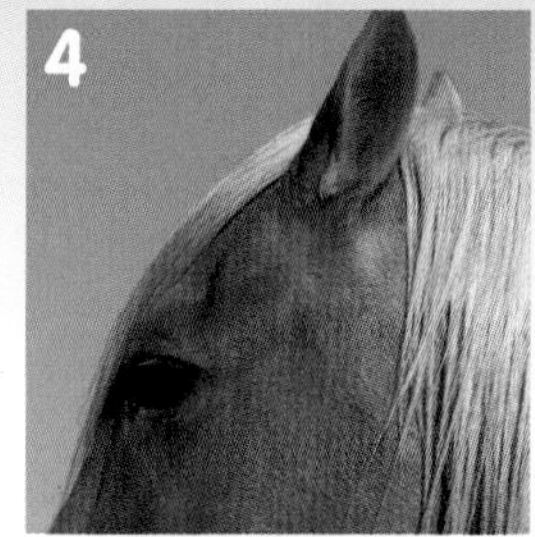
4

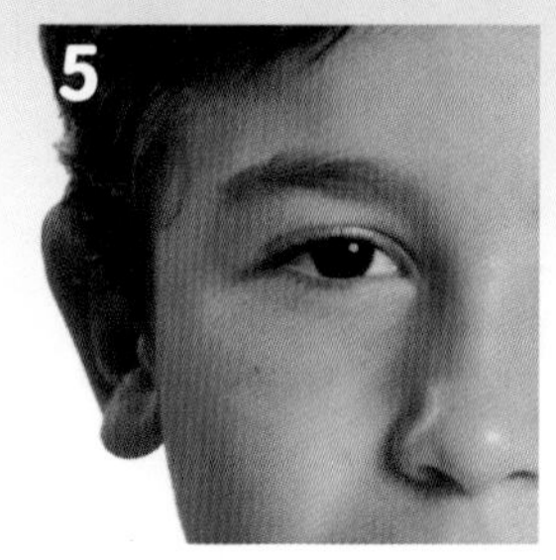
5

10 Draw and say.

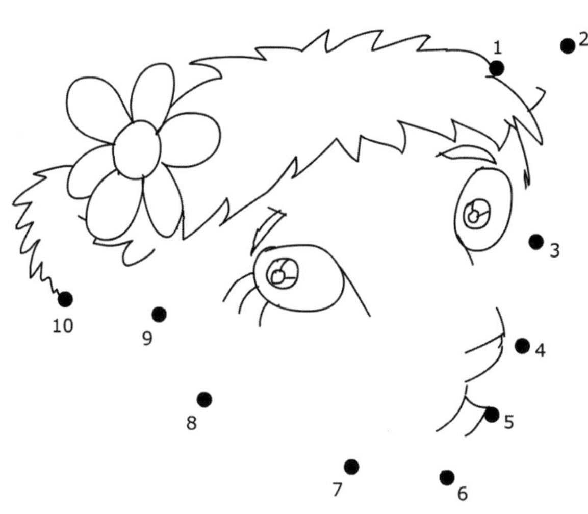

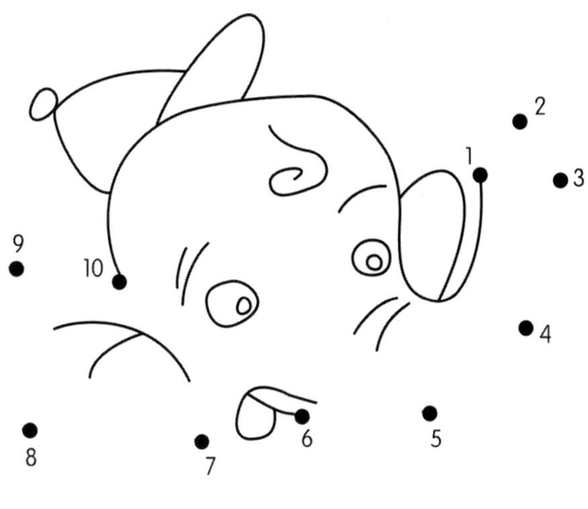

11 Mime and draw. Then say.

My alphabet Pp Qq Rr

1 **Listen and repeat. Then circle.**

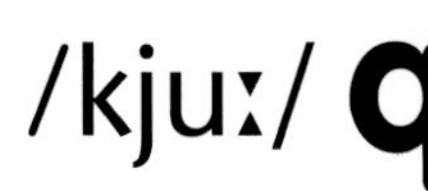

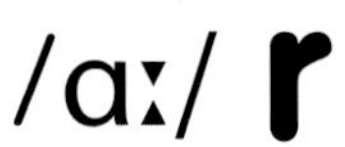

/piː/ p /kjuː/ q /ɑː/ r

/p/ panda /kw/ queen /r/ rabbit

2 **Find and circle.**

/p/	p r q j p q j p g p p j p c p
	P A C P P B C P A P C B P A P
/kw/	q p r q j p q g q b q p q o q
	Q C Q O Q Q P D Q C Q C A Q L
/r/	r c r f r c r r h r n r o c f
	R B R D R F R P R R Q R P C R

3 Find and circle.

p q r

Q p R q

P  r

4 Find and write. Then say.

a b c d e f g h i j k l m n o p q r

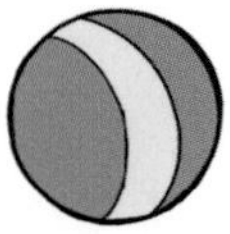

ball dog fish horse ___anda apple ___ar

goat egg ___ueen ___abbit ___onkey ___urse ___range

___ite lorry jelly insect

5 Chant.

A B C D E F G H I J K L M N O P Q R S T U V W X Y Z
a b c d e f g h i j k l m n o p q r s t u v w x y z

12 Pets

1 Listen and point. Then say.

pets

cat

hamster

snake

2 Look and listen.

1
Look! Here's Sally and Pam, her pet. Have you got a pet, Cabu?
A ... what?

2
Here! Look! A book with pets!

3
What's this?
It's a cat.
Oh, look. Here's a hamster and a snake.

4
Cabu. Have you got a pet?
Yes, I've got a parrot!

3 Listen again and say.

4 **Look and match. Then say.**

It's a snake.
1
2
3
4
a
b
c
d

5 **Draw and colour. Then say.**

It's a ...
1
2
3
4

6 **Play.**

What am I?
You're a dog.
No.

7 Listen and stick. Then sing. 

I've got a pet. A pet? A pet?
Yes, it's a cat.
And a … here, and a … there.
Here a …, there a ….
I've got a pet. A pet? A pet?
Yes, it's a cat.

I've got a pet. A pet? A pet?
Yes, it's a dog.
I've got a pet. A pet? A pet?
Yes, it's a snake.
I've got a pet. A pet? A pet?
Yes, it's a bird.

8 Point, ask and say.

What's this?

It's a …

1 

 2 

 3 

4 

5 

9 Listen and circle.

1
yes no
2
yes no
3
yes no
4
yes no
5
yes no

10 Play.

Have you got a cat?
No.
Have you got a snake?
Yes.

11 Draw and colour. Then say.

This is my cat, Sissy.

My alphabet S t u

① **Listen and repeat. Then circle.**

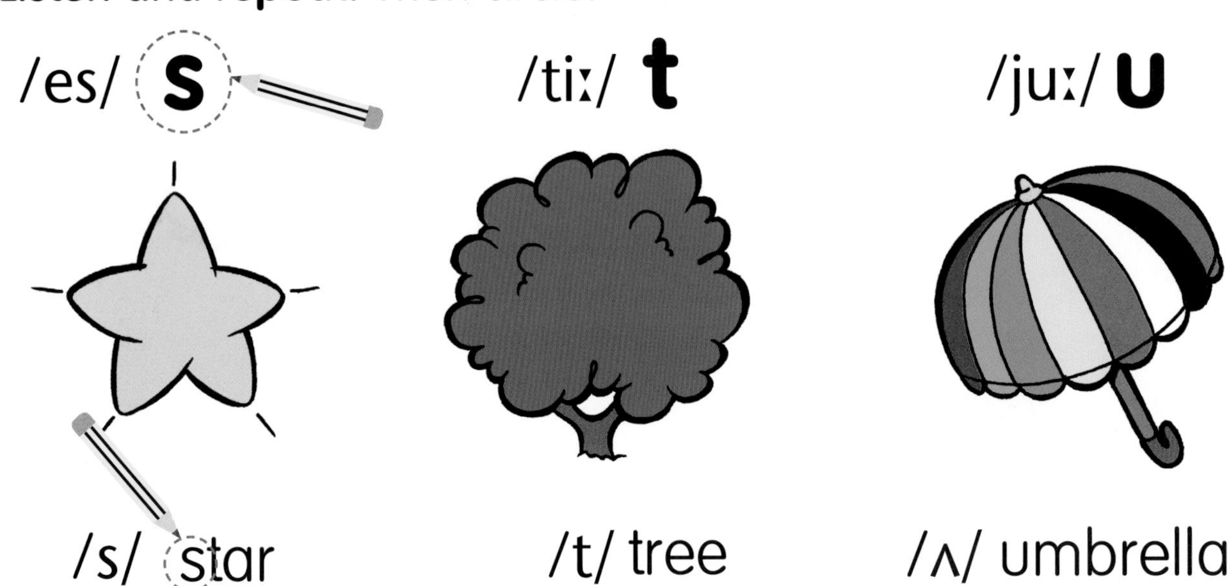

/es/ s
/tiː/ t
/juː/ u
/s/ star
/t/ tree
/ʌ/ umbrella

② **Find and circle.**

/s/	s c s o r s c s s e s a s d c S R S C S S L J S T C S D S O
/t/	t l t b t t i d t f f t f t e h T L F I T T E T N T L E T T J
/ʌ/	u n u i u n o u s u c u a u m U A U B E U H U U K T U U C M

3 Match and say. Then colour.

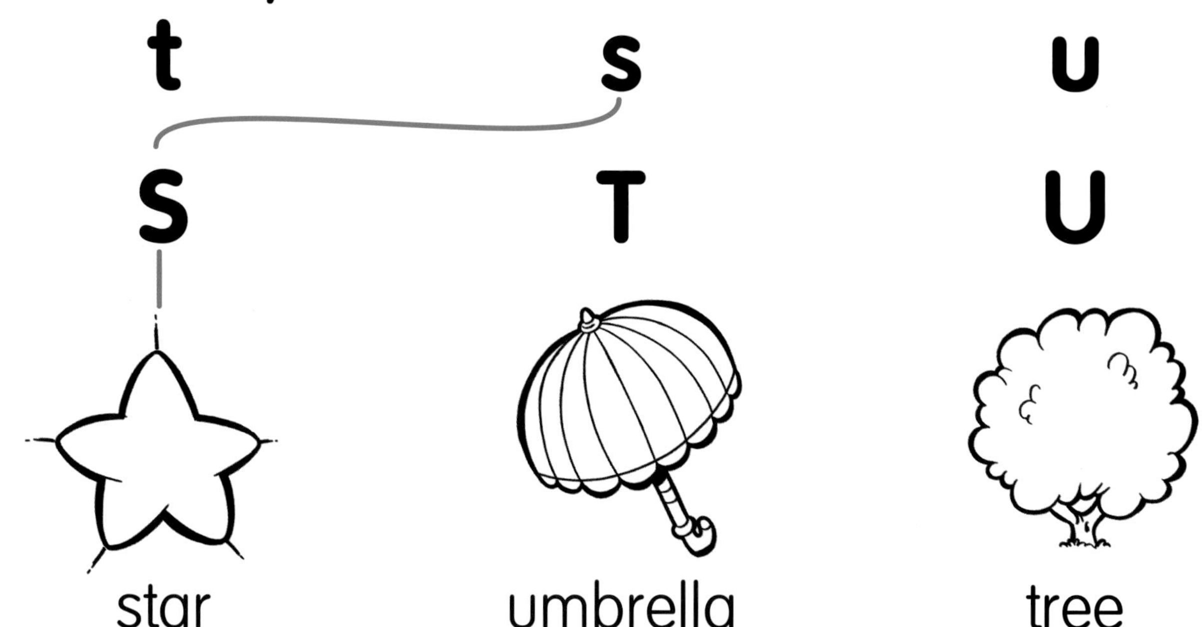

t
s
u
S
T
U
star
umbrella
tree

4 Find and write. Then say.

f
p
n

5 Chant.

A B C D E F G H I J K L M N O P Q R S T U V W X Y Z
a b c d e f g h i j k l m n o p q r s t u v w x y z

13

Food

1 Listen and point. Then say. 

ice cream

chips

salad

burger

2 Look and listen.

1
Yummy! Ice cream.
I like ice cream!
MENU
CHIPS
BURGERS
SALAD
ICE CREAM

2
Look! Chips. I like chips!
MENU
CHIPS
BURGERS
SALAD
ICE CREAM

3
I like salad! Yum!
Yum! ... I like burgers!
I don't like salad.

3 Listen again and say. 

4 Listen and number.

a
1
b
c
d
e

5 Draw ☺ or ☹. Then say.

I like ...

I don't like ...

6 Play.

Ice cream. I like ice cream.

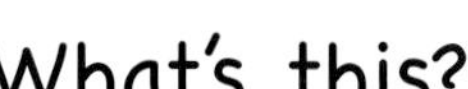

What's this?

PORTOFINO

Listen and stick. Then sing.

I like burgers
Yum, yum!

I don't like chips
No, no!

I like ice cream
Mmm, mmm!

I don't like salad
No, no!

8 Listen and circle.

1

yes no

2

yes no

3

yes no

4

yes no

5

yes no

6

yes no

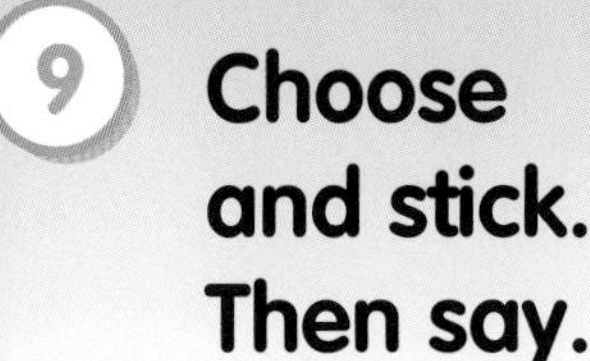

9 **Choose and stick. Then say.**

I like ...

Menu
Menu

10 **Draw and colour.**

11 **Play.**

Salad and chips, please.
Thank you.

My alphabet Vv Ww

1 **Listen and repeat. Then circle.**

/viː/ **v** /ˈdʌbəljuː/ **w**

/v/ violin /w/ watch

2 **Find and circle.**

/v/	v u n v o v c v v e w v r v w
	V W V N V U M V A W V R V A V

/w/	w v u w m w w n w v r w l w v
	W A V W M N W V V W W R W M W

3 Say, look and circle.

4 Find and write. Then say.

5 Chant.

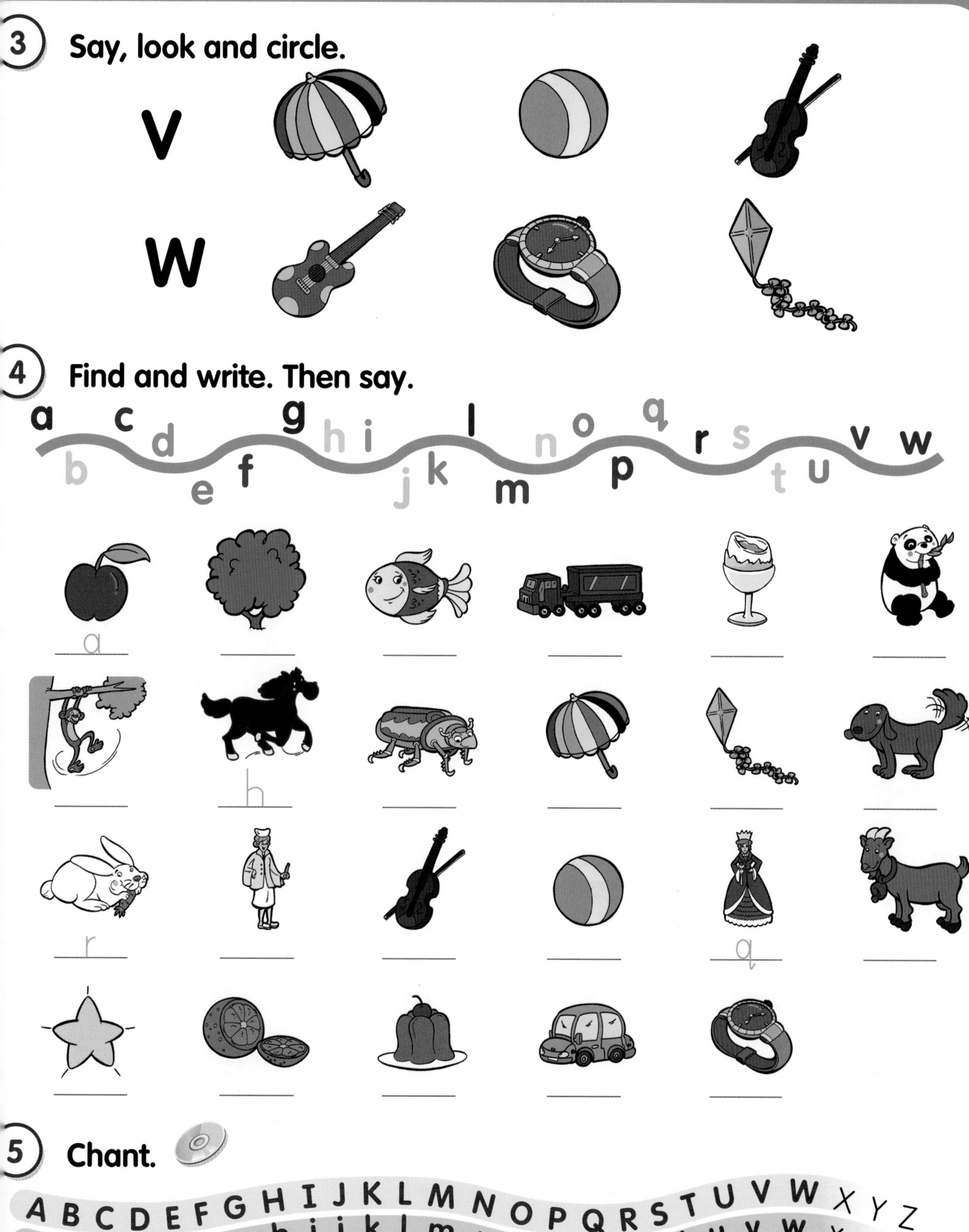
V
W
a c d g h i l n o q r s v w
b e f j k m p t u
a
h
r
q
A B C D E F G H I J K L M N O P Q R S T U V W X Y Z
a b c d e f g h i j k l m n o p q r s t u v w x y z

14 Actions

1 Listen and point. Then say.

fly

jump

swim

run

2 Look and listen.

1
Look! I can fly.
Trumpet! Come on!
Yes, I can fly.

2
Trumpet! Can you jump?
No, I can't.

3
Come on, Trumpet! Can you swim?
Yes, I can.
I can jump.

4
I can run and I can fly!
No, Trumpet. Run.
Look! I can jump.

3 Listen again and say.

4 Listen and circle.

1

yes no

2

yes no

3

yes no

5 Point and say.

I can ... I can't ...

1

2

3

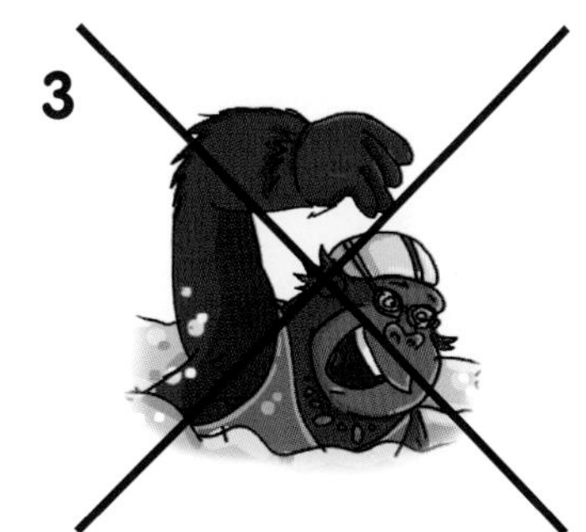

4

6 Play.

Can you jump?

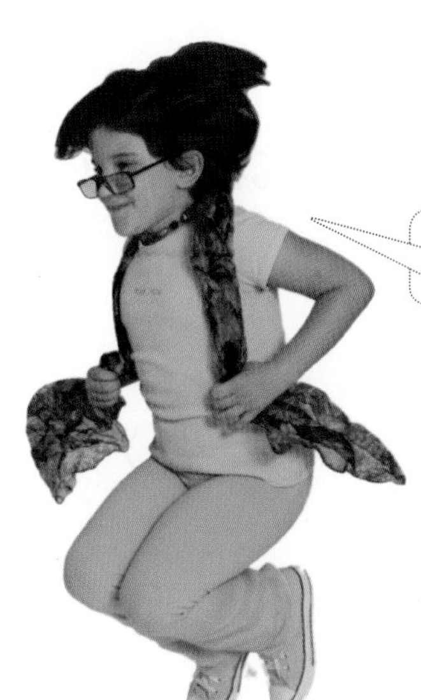

Yes, I can. Look!

7 Listen and stick. Then sing. 

Can you jump?
Yes, I can.

Can you fly?
No, I can't.

I'm Cabu.
I can jump.
I can jump!

Can you fly?
Yes, I can.

Can you swim?
No, I can't.

I'm Paco.
I can fly.
I can fly!

8 Play. Who am I?

Can you swim?
No, I can't.
Can you fly?
Yes, I can.
You're Paco.
Yes!

9 Look and circle. Then say.

I can ...

I can't ...

1 yes no

2 yes no

3 yes no

4 yes no

5 yes no

6 yes no

10 Play.

Can you swim?

Yes, I can.

My alphabet

1 Listen and repeat. Then circle.

/eks/ **x** /waɪ/ **y** /zed/ **z**

/ks/ fox /j/ yo-yo /z/ zebra

2 Find and circle.

/ks/	x y v x w x e x x e y z x v x
	X A Y X W X V X K X X Z X A K
/j/	y z y x v y k y w y u y w v y
	Y X V Y Y W Z Y A Y K Y W Y X
/z/	z v x z u w z z y z x z u z v
	Z X Z Y N Z W N Z A Z Z X M Z

3 Say, look and circle.

4 Find and say. Then match and colour.

X
Y
Z
a b c d e f g h i
z j
y k
x l
w m
v u t s r q p o n

5 Chant.

A B C D E F G H I J K L M N O P Q R S T U V W X Y Z
a b c d e f g h i j k l m n o p q r s t u v w x y z

JUNGLE FUN 3

1 Stick and say.

I've got a big nose and two small eyes.

1

2

3

4

2 Draw. Then play.

3 Match, draw and colour. Then say.

I like ...

I don't like ...

Goodbye!

1 Look and listen.

1
Hello. I'm Cabu. This is Trumpet and this is Paco.
Hello, Cabu. Hello, Trumpet and Paco. I'm Sally.

2
Look, Sally! I can fly!
I can jump.
Look! I've got a hamster!

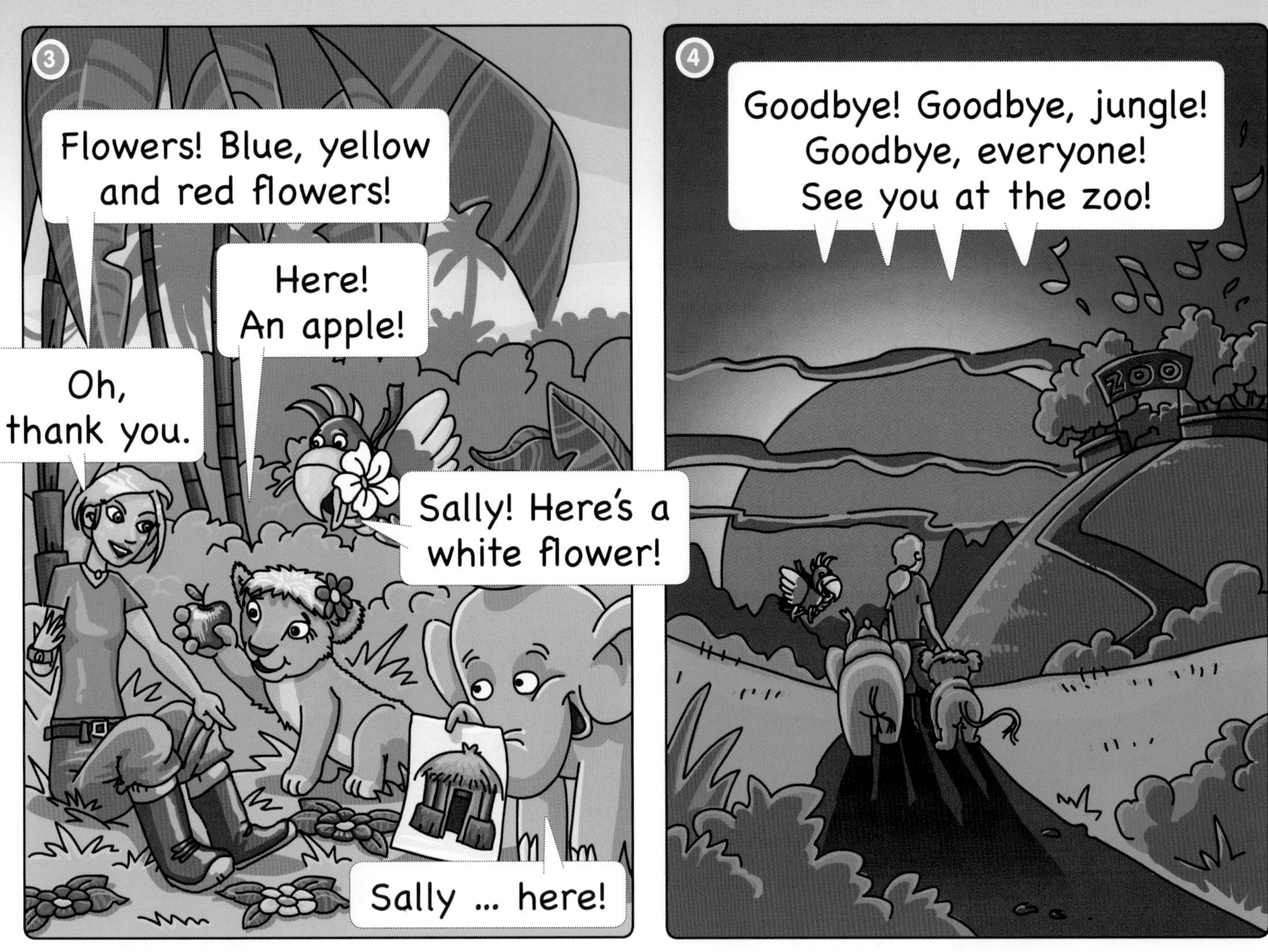
3
Flowers! Blue, yellow and red flowers!
Here! An apple!
Oh, thank you.
Sally! Here's a white flower!
Sally ... here!
4
Goodbye! Goodbye, jungle! Goodbye, everyone! See you at the zoo!
ZOO

2 **Listen again and say.**

3 **Sing.**

Goodbye, Cabu.
Goodbye, Trumpet.
Thank you! Thank you!
Goodbye, Paco.

Happy Christmas!

1 Listen and point. Then say. 

present

Father Christmas

stocking

2 Look and listen. 

 **Listen again and say.** 

 **Sing.** 

Merry Christmas, Merry Christmas!
Look at the presents and the tree.

Merry Christmas, Merry Christmas!
Here's your present, with love from me!

Merry Christmas, Merry Christmas!
Open your stocking, look and see!

Thank you! Thank you! Thank you!
Merry Christmas!

 **Draw a Christmas card.**

Happy
Christmas!

Happy Easter!

1 **Listen and point. Then say.** 

Easter Bunny

egg

basket

2 **Look and listen.** 

3 **Listen again and say.**

4 **Find and count. Then colour.**

My Picture Dictionary

1 In the jungle

lion elephant parrot boy girl

banana flower bee hippo

2 Colours (1)

yellow blue red green

3 Numbers 1–5

 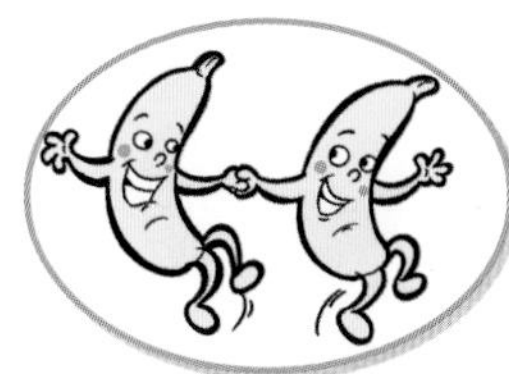   

one two three four five

4 In the classroom

a b c

teacher desk chair book door

5 School things

bag pencil crayon rubber

6 Classroom actions

sit down stand up clap turn around

7 Family

mum dad brother sister me

8 Toys

train plane bike guitar

9 Colours (2)

pink black orange white

10 Numbers 6–10

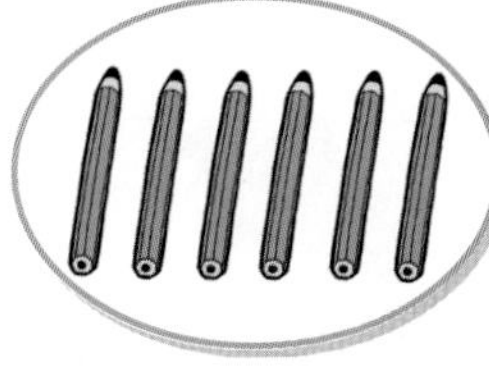 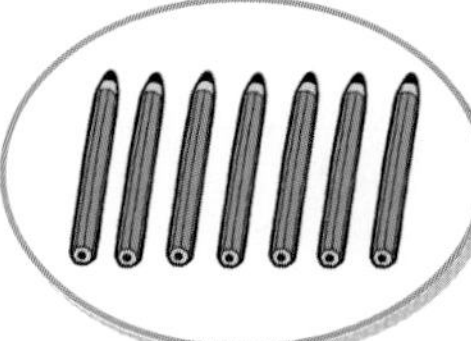 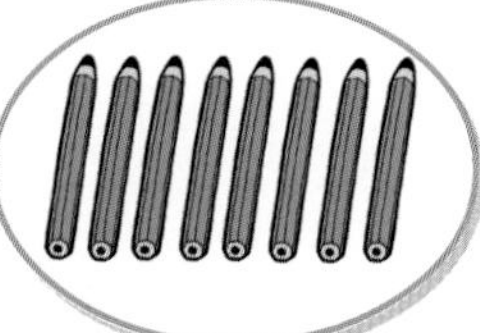 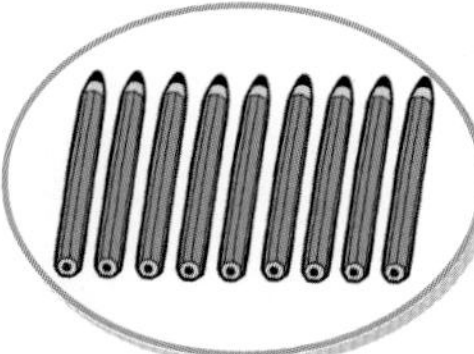 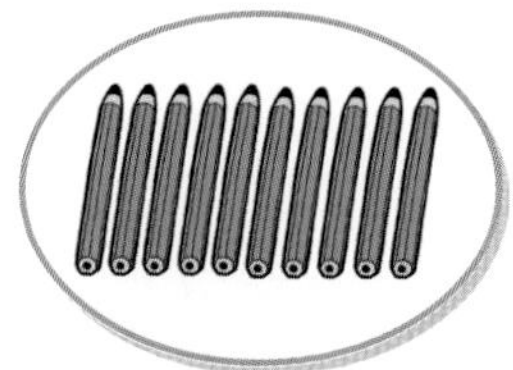

six seven eight nine ten

11 Face

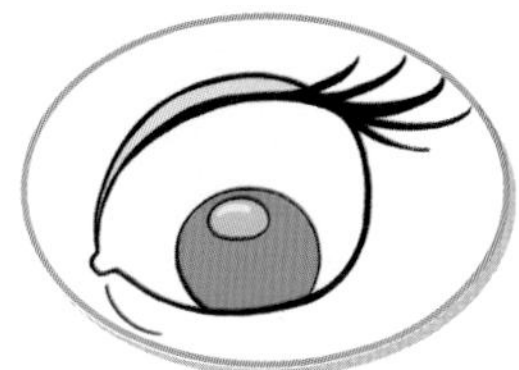 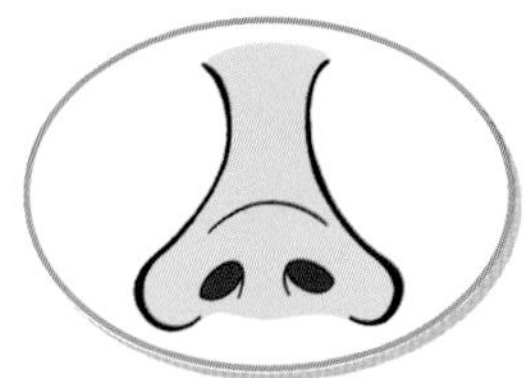 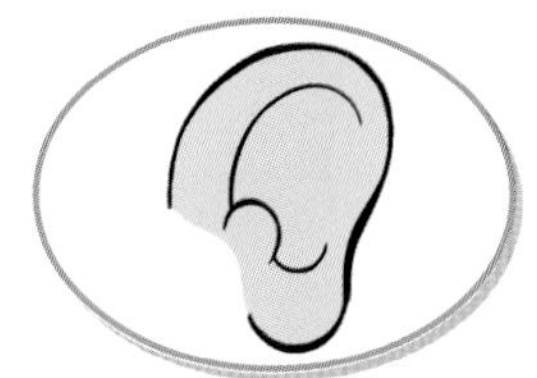 

eye nose ear mouth

12 Pets

pets cat hamster snake

13 Foods

ice cream chips salad burger pizza

14 Actions

fly jump swim run

Happy Christmas! Happy Easter!

   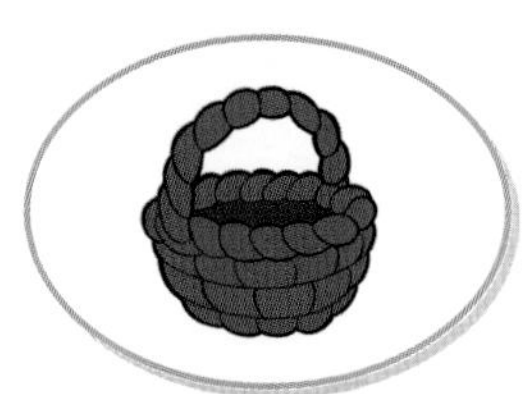

present stocking egg basket

My Alphabet

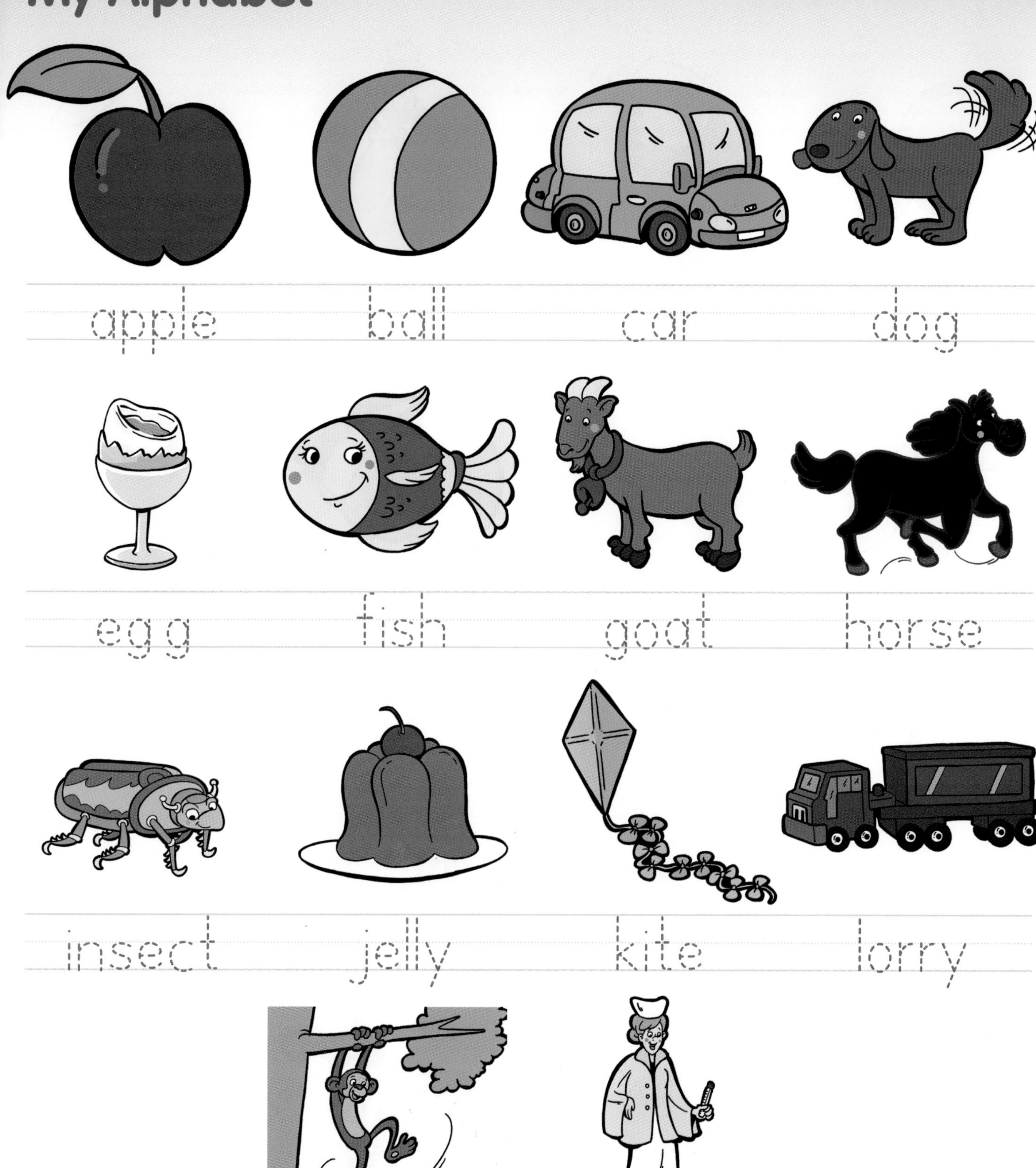
apple
ball
car
dog
egg
fish
goat
horse
insect
jelly
kite
lorry

monkey nurse

My Alphabet

orange panda queen rabbit

star tree umbrella violin

watch fox

yo-yo zebra

page 16

page 24

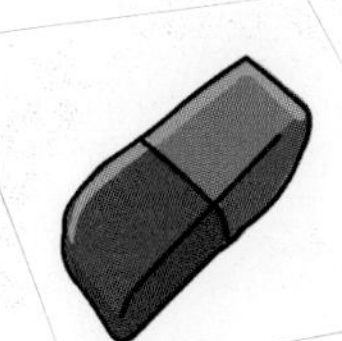

page 36

page 42

page 48

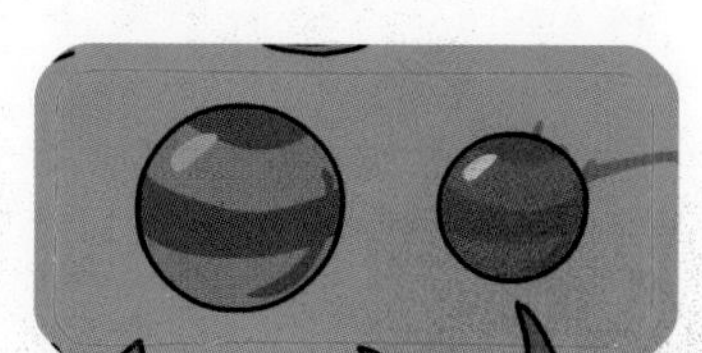

page 54

page 68

page 74

page 75

page 80

page 84

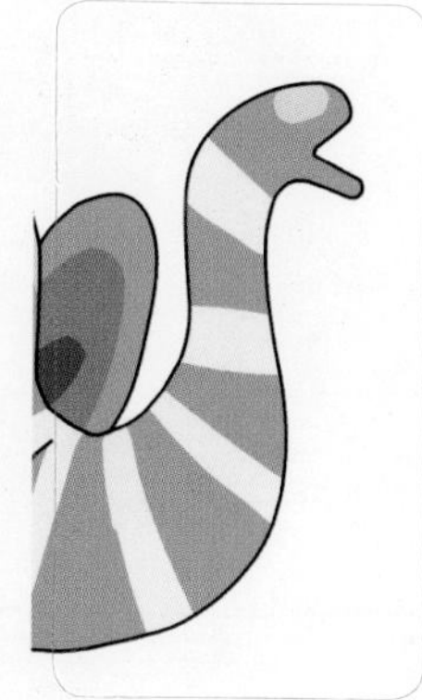